FRONTLINE

BROTHERS

S/SGT Rick Barnes

Edited by: Annalisa Sawick

Published in the United States of America.
First edition December 2021.

Front cover photo of Second Platoon, Fox Company taken
before Operation Union II, courtesy of Mike Hernandez
Book cover design by Flintlock Covers
Editor/Writing Coach: Annalisa Sawick

This is a work of creative nonfiction. The events and
experiences detailed here are all true and have been
faithfully reported as the author has remembered them to
the best of his ability. No names, identities and
circumstances have been changed to protect the privacy
and/or the anonymity of the various individuals involved.
Some have vetted the manuscript and confirmed its
rendering of events.

To request permissions, contact the author at
barnesmarco@earthlink.net

TABLE OF CONTENTS

PROLOGUE

In war stories, names, ranks, and objectives rush past our eyes like bullets on a battlefield; swiftly finding their way to the intended target, without a second thought as to the impact of that fleeting moment in time. That single moment can change history, change lives, take lives, alter your perception of life, despite the war continuing on. Soldiers are more than their names placed on a memorial wall or their unmarked graves that are adorned with a simple flag once a year to honor their sacrifice. Each soldier has a story, a perspective, a life, before that life was thrown into war. Some are even privileged enough to continue life after war, but once you have that experience, there is no going back. You lose more than the brother standing next to you and that loss only amplifies over time. You begin to see that your grief expands far past physically losing someone; it takes the form of a ghostly shadow, hovering over your shoulder. In moments of sadness, it rears its ugly head, compounding your sorrow. In moments of joy, it whispers shrouds of guilt into your ear. It encompasses everything that you have that someone else will never get to experience. That type of grief, love that can no longer be shared, sticks with you for a lifetime and can only be resolved by making peace with living for those that left too soon. This book is for all the untold stories, all the stories behind the history, and all the history that was never had, because the ultimate sacrifice was made.

I hope to do **my brothers** justice in helping others understand that war is a person, not an event. It has its own demons and secrets, it has a face, a name, and a heart far beyond what words on paper could ever portray.

DEDICATION

To my Daughters: Tracie Barnes Hlebasko and Tonya Barnes Devries, who have shown unconditional love regardless of my many weaknesses.

To my Son in Law: Greg Hlebasko, for your perseverance in pushing me for years to write this book.

To my Grandchildren: Andrew & Katie Hlebasko, Nicholas Hlebasko, Olivia Hlebasko, Brooke & Robby Nelson, and Luke Devries, whom I could not be prouder.

To my precious Great Grandchildren: Alina Hlebasko, Jameson Nelson and Raegan Nelson, may you always know me through my stories even when I'm not physically here.

Alina Hlebasko & Jameson Nelson

Raegan Nelson

Left to right: Luke Devries, Olivia Hlebasko, Brooke Devries, Rick Barnes (Author), Andrew Hlebasko, & Nick Hlebasko

WHERE IT ALL BEGAN

"Only the dead have seen the end of war."

-Plato

1.1 *Growing Up Before Vietnam*

Rick Barnes was born September 25, 1947, to Charles and
Pauline Barnes in Arcadia Valley, Missouri. Growing up in
Ironton, the northern parts of the Ozark Mountains, granted
him the opportunity of adventures in a heavily wooded, rural
area. Rick and his brothers wasted no time creating their
own fun along the foothills of Pilot Knob Mountain. Playing
around an old military fort nearby always made their fun and
games more authentic, as if somehow the land attracted
those with an affinity for battle. It was indeed the scene of
one of the largest and hardest fought battles waged on
Missouri soil during the Civil War in September of 1864. The
Battle of Pilot Knob was led by Confederate Major General
Sterling Price, an army of 8,000 men against the Union Post of
Ford Davidson.

Intrigued by the area alone, naive to the vast history below
their feet, the boys would spend hours upon hours, ducking
and weaving through trees. They would strategize the next
attack in their game of "war," holstering their weapons made
of sawed-off broom handles and rubber bands. But soon the
rubber band rifles became too elementary, requiring a more
advanced and realistic form of war that inflicted higher
levels of pain, hence the BB gun era. Every young boy in that
time period had one. They instantly acquired more than their
fair share of red welts, returning home with bloody battle
wounds from a day in the woods. To this day, they still aren't
sure how they emerged from their childhood with both eyes.
Little did he know at the time, but these "games" along with
his Cherokee blood line, would prepare Rick with the skills
he needed for Vietnam and lead to the irrefutable nickname
given to him by his Company, Hawkeye.

Being the middle of five children, three brothers and one
sister, while living on a small farm, led to some fond
childhood memories. There was always at least one dog
running the property as chickens squawked around their

coop. They also had a horse and cow. Rick's chores involved milking the cow and maintaining the ice box. Keeping it cold required numerous trips with his red wagon to the icehouse, loading the bulky blocks, and making the long trek back home. Finding your own entertainment during chore time was an essential part of farm life, but was usually closely followed by reprimands and punishments as Rick would often return home with half a block of ice after his makeshift sledding escapades on the slippery route.

It was playing in and around the iron county area that led to Rick and his brother Bill, contracting polio. Rick's brother wasn't diagnosed with the virus until he was far along into his illness, with Rick being diagnosed two weeks after. This resulted in a two week stay for both brothers at Shriners hospital in St. Louis, Missouri. Both Rick and Bill would be placed side by side in what was called an "Iron Lung." An iron lung was a large negative pressure ventilator which enclosed most of the person's body to regulate the air pressure. It was used to simulate breathing for a person suffering from paralysis. Polio would often cause curvature of the spine which would in turn cause difficulty in breathing.

For Rick, the residual effects from the disease were minor; his brother wasn't so lucky. Bill would undergo numerous surgeries to correct his spine along with having to wear braces and use crutches to walk for the remainder of his life. Polio would lead to Rick and Bill becoming inseparable throughout their school years. You could always find Bill on the handlebars of Rick's bicycle or Rick hanging on the back of Bill's go-kart. Not long after that, their father received a promotion, moving the family to northwest Indiana where Rick would finish the remainder of his middle and high school years.

Highland Indiana in the early 1960s was the perfect place for Rick to fine-tune his hunting skills. He mostly went after rabbits and pheasants with his rifle or bow, which his mother gladly cooked for the family, but absolutely refused to prepare in any other capacity. The cleaning and dressing were left to Rick. These skills would later serve him well as he navigated unknown territory in the face of combat and jungle warfare. Rick did have a few run-ins with the law as a kid, but only due to hunting within the city limits. And Rick's father always came to the rescue; captivating the officers with the history behind his son's weapons, being they were the very same guns he used while traversing the Ozark Mountains of Missouri as a kid himself. Each time, his art of storytelling and persuasion won the station over, and each time, he was able to recover the 22 caliber and 410 shotgun with ease. His father's stories were always entertaining, but they were also true. As they say, the truth shall set you free.

By 1965, Rick was a senior in high school and his curiosity regarding his father's exploits while fighting the Germans in World War II fueled a hunger to learn more about history; one of the few classes he excelled at during school. He became even more intrigued by the Vietnam War that was currently escalating in Indo China. Rick felt the urge to be a part of the subject he had grown an affinity for and began to worry that if he didn't enlist in the military soon, he would miss out on an important opportunity. He wanted to fight for his country as his father had. Rick's older brother, Chuck, had just enlisted in the Marine Corps and was headed to Vietnam. Knowing his brother was already out there only increased his sense of urgency; right after graduation he immediately went to the local Marine Corps recruiter. To his dismay, being that he was 17, he needed permission from both parents to enlist. He wouldn't turn 18 for another month and a half. It took some time, but eventually he was able to convince his parents that if they didn't agree to it now, he'd do it anyway on his 18th birthday. On August 9, 1965, he would officially be welcomed into the United States Marine Corps.

FRONTLINE BROTHERS

Although crippled with polio, Bill rushed to all four branches after hearing of Rick's enlistment, pleading and begging with recruiters to let him be a part of the war in any way possible. His only desire was to serve his country alongside his brothers. Because of his condition, he was rejected and denied entrance into the military; a disappointment he would carry for many years after. Their littlest brother, Pat, was too young to enlist and remained at home while the others deployed; entering the mouth of the enemy with only a fraction of an understanding as to what they were about to encounter. His father later told him that one of the most pitiful sights he's ever witnessed was watching his son's face in the window of the train as it left the station from Chicago. Rick was just a young boy, headed for a man's war.

1.2 *Preparing for a Man's War*

Upon arrival at the Marine Corps Recruit Depot in San Diego, CA for boot camp, you were instantly welcomed with a haircut and the removal of your civilian clothes along with any personal items. The idea was to rid you of your identity as they rebuilt you into the killing machine they desired you to be. Even after training was finished, my only thought was, they have trained me to kill. That's it. That's all I know how to do. How do you pick a job after the war when every skill, thought, and reaction you've been taught for the past four years pertains to killing?

Boot camp was normally 12 weeks but due to the shortage of troops, it was expedited into an eight week program. Training would start at dawn with a five to six mile run, you'd be talked to like dirt, treated like less than dirt, and expected to perform at a level that seemed inhumane. A fear began to grow inside me each day that passed, is this what it's going to be like in the military for the next four years? Is this what I signed up for? I couldn't see past the training. But I somehow chose to continue, trusting that there had to be something more.

You were taught hand-to-hand combat, which included bayonet training. You endured obstacle courses and learned what it was like to be gassed. Hours were spent on the drill field, learning to be a team; a unit. Uniforms were meticulously maintained. No wrinkle or scuff permitted. Anything that was meant to shine was shined. You didn't even own your thoughts anymore because the moment your thoughts interfered with the second nature that was taught, you were dead. That especially applied to military rank. Once you entered Vietnam, you were not to salute officers and no one wore rank insignias. This was to prevent valuable leaders from being identified and targeted by snipers.

Back then, things were done in boot camp that would never be allowed today. On one particular occasion, I went the wrong way during drill formation training. I hastily tried to correct my step, but not before the drill sergeant saw my costly mistake. When we got back to the quonset hut, a metal building where we all lived and slept, I saw the drill sergeant headed towards me, red in the face and far from happy. He stopped directly in front of me, inches from my nose and loudly proclaimed, "You piece of shit! You fucked up today." He quickly looked to his left and right before landing a swift punch to my gut, almost knocking me off my feet. You couldn't make mistakes and you quickly learned the cost of even the smallest misstep.

Sometimes you'd get called to the drill sergeant's hut where he'd yell, "On the locker!" Everyone would have to jump up and hang on the locker for 30 mins to an hour, until he said you could get down. It wouldn't matter how pointless a command seemed, what mattered was that you obeyed.

Growing up I had a stuttering problem. It persisted throughout my youth and continued into my teenage years as I entered the Marine Corps. One morning I was on the parade deck during our routine inspection, where they made sure you were clean shaven and your uniform was perfect, when the drill sergeant stopped in front of me, "What is your name turd?" I began stuttering in response, suddenly unable to control the movements of my mouth when they mattered most. His booming voice reverberated between my ears, "You piece of shit! Can't you fucking talk!? How'd you get into this Corps if you can't even talk!?" After that, I never stuttered again. The Marines literally scared the stutter right out of me.

In the Marines, you are taught an entirely different set of vocabulary words. A "cherry" or a virgin, is what they called the new recruits and if you were "sandbagging" you were shirking your duties. When you were marching it was called "humping" and anyone manning a typewriter was considered to be a "Remington Raider." A "hooch" was a Vietnamese dwelling, "in-country" meant you were in Vietnam and the United States was considered the "real world." And after 15 months in Vietnam, I became a "booney rat." The enemy was known as a "Charlie" or "dink" and Asians were "gooks." There was a sense of racial hatred infused into conversations and training, especially as American casualties in Vietnam grew. The racial slurs only escalated as drill instructors returned from combat in Vietnam to train recruits. Killing a person was not a normal instinct for a recruit, or really any person for that matter. It was something that had to be taught. And in order to teach someone to kill another human, they needed to instill hate. We needed to hate the people we were fighting so there was no remorse when we were killing. The only problem with that, is after boot camp, you thought you were the baddest motherfucker that ever-walked God's green earth, so getting into fights was fairly common. There was no turning off the kill switch. Your desire to fight was tightly wound around the self-discipline that had been drilled into your every movement.

After completing boot camp, I was sent to Camp Pendleton in California for infantry and M60 machine gun school. There, you became proficient in a Military Occupational Specialty or MOS. For four weeks you attended ITR or Infantry Training Regiment and learned advanced training in the use of weapons and combat maneuvers. This included two weeks of training in your MOS, for me, it was machine gun school (0331). By the end of school, not only had I learned how to fire my weapon, but I could dismantle it in seconds and knew how to clean every inch. In fact, by the end of training, you knew how to disassemble and assemble the machine gun blindfolded.

My first duty assignment was to report to the Fox Company, Second Battalion, Fifth Marines Regiment. I had no idea it was the most decorated battalion in Marine Corps history, with Fox Company having the most distinction of all. Any Marine at the time would tell you that no one wanted to be sent to the Second Battalion, let alone be assigned to Fox Company. A battalion and company with that kind of notoriety when arriving in Vietnam would volunteer for every tough assignment available; Fox had a reputation to maintain and uphold.

In early February of 1966, we headed to Camp Schwab in northern Okinawa for counter-guerrilla warfare school. The company conducted extensive field training which included day and night live firing techniques, efficient use of sniper scopes, instruction in land mines, demolition, and training in the use of helicopters. There was no down time; you were always on. There was no time to sit and reflect on what all this extensive training in guerilla warfare meant on the front lines, there was just the mission; the mission to get there. What happened after getting there wasn't at the forefront of anyone's thoughts. They were just living day to day and developing their instincts for survival. Once the men hit the shores of the Chu Lai combat base aboard the USS Clymber, we felt lucky to be given the opportunity for additional training. It was later believed that access to this extensive training program in Okinawa was responsible for the survival of numerous soldiers. It had provided them with effective strategies for combat, the knowledge to counteract the enemies homefield advantage and style of warfare, and it had allowed their escape from countless near-death situations. I firmly believe it was one of the reasons I survived my two tours in Vietnam.

Machine Gun School

"Junk on the Bunk" inspection at Camp Schwab, Okinawa

1.3 *The Fifth Marine Regiment*

There are thousands of numbered units throughout the military, many with extensive histories and combat roles since the United States military began operating on the world stage. The U.S. Army's Third Infantry Regiment can trace its lineage all the way back to the American Revolution. The First Infantry Division lays claim to the longest, continuously serving division in the U.S. military. Even the Navy has the famed USS Constitution, the oldest commissioned sailing ship in the fleet. However, no unit has been deployed to every major conflict over the last 100 years except for one, the Fifth Marine Regiment.

The Fifth Marine Regiment's story begins on June 8, 1917, when it was activated in Philadelphia as part of the United States build-up for World War I. The regiment was assigned to the Fourth Marine Brigade, which became part of the U.S. Army's Second Division. The Fifth would establish itself in Marine Corps history for its actions at the Battle of Belleau Wood in the spring of 1918.

During the regiment's service in France, it earned its nickname, "The Fighting Fifth" and was awarded the French Fourragere for receiving three Croix de Guerre citations; a decoration that members of the Fifth Marines wear to this day. During these campaigns, five Marines and one Navy Corpsman received the Medal of Honor.

The next major action for the Fighting Fifth was battling their way across the Pacific in World War II. The Fifth landed on Guadalcanal on August 7, 1942, and endured grueling combat for four months before being relieved with the rest of the division on December 9, 1942. For their efforts, the Fifth Marines and the entire First Marine Division received their first Presidential Unit Citation.

18

The Fifth Marines entered combat on Peleliu on September 15, 1944. Unbeknownst to them, the Japanese had changed their tactics from attempting to stop landings at the beach, to fortifying the entire island and creating a defense at depth. The lack of this knowledge would cost the Marines dearly. After the seizure of the airfield, the rest of the division set out to clear the remainder of the island. By late October, the Fifth Marines were the only regiment still combat effective.

The Fifth Marines' final action in World War II took place in Okinawa. The fight on Okinawa made places like Sugar Loaf Hill and Shuri Castle, world renowned. During World War II, four Marines were awarded the Medal of Honor.

War soon found the Fifth Marines deployed to the Pusan Perimeter in the South Korean War. That winter, the Fifth Marines fought for their lives at the "Frozen Chosen" Reservoir. When the situation looked bleak and the Marines were falling back, General Oliver Smith told his command, "Retreat? Hell! We're not retreating, we're just advancing in a different direction." The Fifth Marines held off the Chinese's attempts to break the main line of resistance until the armistice in July 1953. The heroic actions of the Fifth Marines earned 10 more Medals of Honor and another Presidential Unit Citation.

Peacetime didn't last long for the Fighting Fifth. Just over a decade after leaving Korea, PFC Rick Barnes was part of the troop buildup in Vietnam in May 1966. Corporal Barnes went on to fight alongside his Marine brothers in Fox company, Second Platoon for the next 15 months. The Fifth Marines spent six years battling the North Vietnamese Army and the Viet Cong. During the Vietnam War, seven members of the regiment received the Medal of Honor before returning to Camp Pendleton in 1971. Corporal Barnes served in combat alongside two of those Marines; one under his leadership, the other, his Commanding Officer.

1.4 *Arrival in Vietnam*

On April 8, 1966, Rick Barnes left Okinawa aboard the *USS George Clymber* with the Second Battalion, Fifth Marines, First Marine Division. *The Clymber* was a Middleton-class attack transport ship. The ship had been commissioned during World War II and the Korean War and was now being used in the Vietnam War. The transport ship arrived off the shore of South Vietnam at Chu Lai on April 13, 1966. The debarkation of Marines was achieved with a landing craft (LCM) and done in the same fashion as in previous wars by loading the troops using a net along the ship's side. It was later realized that this procedure was done not only as a method to get the troops onto the beaches of Chu Lai, but also as a training exercise for debarking transport ships in the past.

Rick aboard the USS Clymber, South China Sea

*Fox Company troops aboard LMC (Landing Craft) headed for
Chu Lai Beach*

The Second Battalion, Fifth Marines (2/5) tactical area of
operation was assigned to setting up a command post on Hill
69 and providing airfield defense around the area of Chu Lai.
The normal problems of a newly arrived organization were
blatantly evident and setting up as an operating organization
was compounded by the initial splitting up of the command
group. It didn't help that the battalion's equipment was still
being offloaded from shipping, causing a logistical problem;
it didn't catch up with the battalion until ten days later.
During the latter part of April, 2/5 exchanged a number of
officers and men with units of the Seventh and First Marine
Regiment for the purpose of spreading out the newly arrived
Marines. As chaotic as this was in establishing a cohesive
unit, it did allow the 2/5 to receive significantly more
combat-ready and experienced Marines that had already
been in-country.

The main objective of 2/5 in its first couple months in Vietnam, was to take a green, untried military unit and mold it into an efficient, fighting machine. During the rest of April and most of May, Fox Company would be under the operational control of the Chu Lai defense command. The company went through a period of acclimating itself to not only the climate, but also the novel combat situations they encountered. This would be achieved through aggressive patrolling and ambushing throughout the first few months in Vietnam. By June 1966, Fox company had effectively adjusted to the terrain and combat style of the enemy and would continue to operate aggressively within the assigned tactical area of operation. By July, this had enabled Fox Company's officers and men to acquire a great deal of combat experience.

During the afternoon of April 28, PFC Barnes, along with his machine gun team, were part of a Sparrow Hawk reactionary force to help extract a squad of Marines that were pinned down. They were south of Hill 69, in an area that was called "VC Valley" by the Marines. It was the first heavy firefight Barnes had been engaged in since his arrival in Vietnam. They remained engaged for over two hours. There were two confirmed enemy KIA's (Killed In Action) with numerous blood trails surrounding the area. The Marines escaped the firefight with no casualties, a feat worthy of celebration.

Barnes with machine gun, taken right after first firefight

INTO THE EYE OF THE STORM

"The war in Vietnam was a fluid one with no front lines. The enemy was tough, versatile, tenacious, and cunning. He possessed strong entrenchments in the villages, mountain hideouts, and jungle redoubts. He was difficult to find and identify...they proved a formidable enemy."

-Lt. Gen. Willard Pearson

2.1 *Mail Call*

While in Vietnam, Corporal Barnes would be faced with the decision to stay in Vietnam or go home, not once, but twice. The initial time presented itself the first week of June 1966. Rick's brother, Lance Corporal Chuck Barnes, was stationed at the postal division in Chu Lai, Vietnam. In the military, everyone has a role; one isn't more important than the other, they all function as vital pieces of a much larger machine. Without certain parts, the machine wouldn't run. And it's important to note that to get one soldier on the front lines, it took about nine support personnel to get them there. With that being said, Rick's brother, Lance Corporal Chuck Barnes, had one of the most important jobs in Vietnam, delivering hope through letters from home. The men valued mail more than anything. Regardless of race, sex or rank, correspondence from the outside world was a glimpse into a dimension so far removed from the one they currently inhabited; one that was far more humane and benevolent.

In Vietnam, the time it took to write a letter without interruption was difficult to come by. Between the nightly defensive perimeter patrols and the darkness that enveloped the jungle, a Marine was able to squeeze in only a few minutes on their breaks; writing under the light of the moon. Stamps were never needed to ensure the letters were delivered home, when "FREE" was written where the stamp was normally placed. Envelopes weren't required either, those luxuries were unavailable in the middle of the jungle. Oftentimes Marines would write on anything they could find, even a piece of cardboard from the box that held their c-rations. C-rations or "combat meals" were developed in 1938 to sustain troops during World War II. They usually consisted of some type of meat-and-hash combo with a pack of cigarettes. And if you were one of the lucky ones like Barnes, who didn't smoke, all you had to do was holler, "Cigarettes!" and a c-ration can of the highly desirable peaches would come flying your way. The Marines that ended up with the ham and lima bean meal would often rather go hungry than consume that option. The c-ration cans could also be used to create a makeshift stove to heat up coffee and cocoa with the help of a P-38; the handiest tool invented by the Marine Corps during World War II. They would use the folding can opener to poke two holes in the side and scrounge a pinch of C4 as a source for heat. Marines would wear the tool around their neck with their dog tags, many veterans still carry one today.

A nice break from the c-rations were the goody packages that would sometimes arrive from family in the mail. Despite being tossed around for 3-4 weeks in the hot weather, every morsel of the crumbled cookies or cakes were passed around and consumed by the Marine. Resupply would come every three to five days, arriving by helicopter in a small clearing on the jungle floor. To the Marines, this was the most important thing to happen all day. Everyone hovered around the Huey helicopter as the company clerk jumped out; a large, canvas bag slung over his shoulder with "U.S. MAIL" in bold letters, stenciled on the side. He looked more like Santa Claus delivering presents rather than a Marine delivering mail.

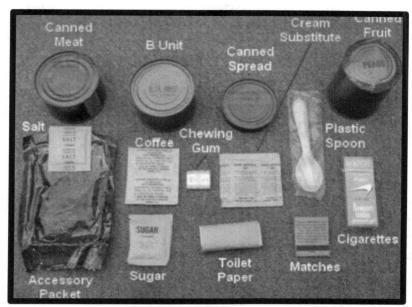

Picture of c-rations

Rick Barnes' dog tags with the P-38 opener

The Marine would listen intently for their names to be called. Pictures and good news were shared openly, entrusting their dreams and fears with one another. Some of the letters would arrive with a hint of perfume, which was passed around so everyone could relish in the sweet scent of their beloved from back home. Letters from wives and girlfriends were read over and over, dozens of times, sometimes even shared amongst each other.

One such time was when Barnes and his best friend, Hank "Ski" Janachowski, were sitting on a pile of sandbags, going through their mail. Ski had just opened a letter he had received earlier that day and turned to Barnes with a smirk. "Hey Barney, do you think it's possible to be in love with someone you've never met?"

Ski had been writing back and forth with a girl named Pat for quite some time now. Knowing that what initially started as a pen pal relationship had transformed into something more, Rick laughed. "Ski, you have let me read some of her letters...if you aren't in love, I am."

Those letters were the beginning of a lifelong love affair that eventually led to the creation of a beautiful family for his friend Ski.

Rick Barnes and Hank "Ski" Januchowski sitting on bunk

Some letters the Marines received were saved, but most were burned or buried so the enemy couldn't retrieve one from a Marines dead body and used to inflict further pain on the Marines' family.

Not all news from home was necessarily good. Some Marines would receive news of a family member or a loved one passing away. While others would begrudgingly open the occasional "Dear John" letter from their girlfriend, fiancé or wife, letting them know that they met someone else and the relationship was over. Marines would fight hard in the hopes of seeing whatever girl they left behind, so to receive this type of news in the middle of war was by far the most disheartening.

During the first week of June, Rick received a letter from his brother stating he was going to catch a chopper to Hill 69 where Fox Company was stationed on perimeter defense under the operational control of the Chu Lai command. The day his brother Chuck arrived to the battalion landing zone, he hopped down from the Huey with nicely pressed jungle fatigues and a brand new M-14 straight from the armory. Rick looked down at his own tattered and ripped fatigues, covered in red clay from traversing the jungle, reeking of body odor and the smell of battle, wondering what his brother thought upon seeing him. The Marines in Fox Company would wear their fatigues until they couldn't be worn anymore and there was hardly any time to wash them or be concerned about appearances; the more you blended into the jungle, the better.

Rick took his brother down to his bunker on the perimeter and introduced him to the other two guys on the machine gun team. Chuck had agreed to stay overnight and catch the mail chopper back to Chu Lia the following day. That evening, Rick and his brother sat on the sandbags in front of the bunker, talking well into the night.

"What unit is in front of your position?" his brother had asked at one point.

Rick looked towards the darkness, "There's nothing out there," while pointing beyond the concertina wire in front of their position, "except the enemy." It was evident on his brother's face that this was the closest he had been to danger or the enemy since his arrival to Vietnam.

Rick looked down at his brother's rifle leaning against the sandbags, "Do you have a round chambered?"

With a look of confusion and genuine concern his brother responded, "No. We never do inside the base at Chu Lai."

Nodding toward Chuck's M-14, Rick gave him the best advice he could at the time, "Well brother, you better lock and load. We get probed on our perimeter or sniper fire almost every night." Lifting his rifle from the sandbags, Chuck chambered a round.

After hours of swapping stories and realizing they needed to get some sleep, Chuck felt compelled to say one more thing, "Rick, an order just came down from the division that no two brothers have to serve in a combat zone at the same time. I'm staying in Chu Lai for the duration of my combat tour. It's safe where I'm at. You should put in a request to return stateside. It's pretty dangerous out here where you're at."

With a resolute look towards his brother and an unwavering finger pointed behind him, Rick replied, "You are my brother by birth, but those are my brothers also inside that bunker. There is no way that I could live with myself walking away from them not serving my due time in this place. I will be staying. Now the decision is yours."

The next morning, Rick walked with his brother to the LZ or landing zone to say goodbye as he caught his ride back to Chu Lai. While watching the chopper lift off, he only hoped he would live to see his brother again.

2.2 *The Lucky Three*

First three confirmed kills, June 11, 1966.

Sometimes war desensitizes you, numbs you, blinds you and you become indifferent in reference towards the actions you are taking or have taken towards another human being. You experience a sense of euphoria when you have survived a situation over the enemy. You are alive; you win. You stop seeing them as a person the moment they are deemed the enemy. The troubling question that would come up after the fact was, "I Just killed and I am happy about it, does that mean I like killing?"

During the month of June, Fox Company was assigned the Tactical Area of Responsibility (TAOR) to include patrolling and maintaining security for Second Battalion, Fifth Marines command post on Hill 69. Hill 69 was named for its feet above sea level on the contour map. The Marines on Hill 69 were not only protecting the battalion command post but also the battalion artillery installations. These locations always seemed to be a target for the Viet Cong sappers or combatants. Most sappers were members of the specially trained Elite North Vietnamese Army Assault Force, Bo Doi Dac Cong, roughly translated, soldiers in special forces. They would camouflage into the night with their bodies covered in charcoal dust and grease, wearing nothing but a pair of black shorts, carrying a satchel filled with explosives. Their objective was to get the loaded satchel into a bunker or artillery gun emplacement and blow it up. Many sappers would take barbiturate tablets or inject themselves with some form of stimulant before rushing towards their destination. On Hill 69 every 50 meters was a sandbagged perimeter bunker that contained three to four Marines. M-60 Machine gun emplacements were strategically located throughout the perimeter to give an effective field of fire.

Bunker on Hill 69

PFC Barnes, Lance Corporal Januchowski, PFC Osborne and PFC Asbell were all located in one of those bunkers (pictured above). PFC Barnes had drawn the 10 to 12 Midnight watch, nothing in 'Nam was more boring than guarding the artillery installations. Barnes was anxious to get back out into the bush where he thought the action was.

Night after night, Barnes would stare out into the darkness with nothing to look at except for those damn rolls of concertina wire lining each bunker. On the evening of June 11, Barnes was the machine gunner with Lance Corporal Januchowski as the team leader. After being awakened promptly at 10:00 PM, Barnes made the visual checks of his machine gun, a full bandolier of ammo was properly chambered. Shortly after taking up position on his usual watch, he heard a *pop!* Suddenly, six Viet Cong sappers were lit up directly in front of him. One of them must have triggered an illumination grenade that Barnes had placed in the concertina wire only a week prior. Grabbing the handle of his M-60 machine gun, Barnes pointed it at the very center, the burst of fire produced a tremendous explosion. He questioned for an instant whether he was shooting bullets or bombs. Realizing he had struck and blown a satchel charge carried by one of the sappers, he knew it wasn't him that they wanted, but the artillery guns to his rear. The explosion had awakened his gun team and Lance Corporal Januchowski who was immediately at his side with a 100-round bandolier of ammo, ready to place in the gun's receiver.

Scanning quickly, Barnes picked his next target, an image running towards a deep well that had been dug by Vietnamese villagers. Just as a burst of fire erupted from his gun the Viet Cong dove for the well and Barnes wasn't sure if his rounds had made contact. Before he had time to think any further, another sapper appeared in his field of vision, attempting to flee the gun fire. Barnes quickly readjusted and sent a couple of long bursts in that direction, knowing he had made contact instantly. As he began scanning for the next target, the illumination grenade expanded and everything went dark; an eerie quiet settling over the area. Everything was over in seconds.

Artillery opened up with illumination canisters periodically until daylight. The area beyond the wire also had been hit with a volley of 81-mm mortars from our command post position. This caused a couple of the village hooches beyond the wire to catch on fire, helping to keep the area illuminated for awhile. No one got any sleep for the rest of the night, Barnes and the machine gun team waited anxiously but no second attack came.

At first light, Barnes immediately volunteered to be a part of a patrol to circle the wire, checking for any dead or wounded. He had to know the fate of the sapper who had jumped into the well.

After circling the wire, three confirmed KIA's were identified. One of the sappers was found dead at the bottom of the 50 foot well, another with only his lower torso intact, his head some 50 feet from his body, and the final, riddled with bullets. These images would follow Corporal Barnes for the next year, especially at night, when he sat in a fox hole waiting for the enemy to come.

In late August, Fox Company would rotate into perimeter duty again on Hill 69 with the bunker positions on the opposite side of the hill this time around. Barnes had moved into the role of team leader for the gun team. After Barnes' experience earlier that June, he felt it was imperative that every Marine under his command stay awake while on watch in the bunker or fox hole. It wasn't just his life that depended on it, but the safety and well-being of every Marine at that command post. He would often awaken in the middle of the night and check to make sure the team member on watch was awake and alert as well. On one particularly quiet evening, Barnes awoke and checked the gun position. It was apparent that his assistant gunner on the team, PFC Phil Hollins, who was supposed to be on watch, had fallen asleep; his head resting on a nearby sandbag, rifle propped up against his body. As Barnes looked out into the night, he decided that this moment was going to be a lesson PFC Hollins would never forget, hopefully sparing his life one day, given the many stories circulating around the company regarding the fate of Marines who were found asleep by the enemy. Barnes slowly pointed the muzzle of his M-14 rifle towards the sandbag near PFC Hollins' head, as the round exploded, the blast echoed throughout the valley. Barnes immediately hollered to let the other Marines know everything was ok as PFC Hollins hastily stood, stunned from the abrupt interruption of sleep, looking beyond frightened, eyes still frantically searching the night for the enemy.

Barnes leaned over and whispered, "If you ever fall asleep

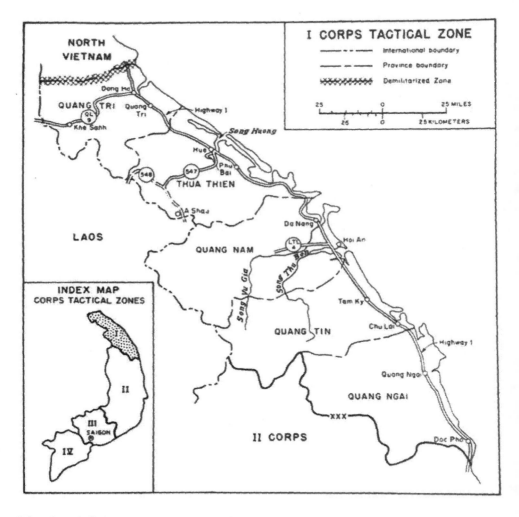

Map from: *US Marines in Vietnam, Fighting the North Vietnamese, 1967*

on my watch again, the next bullet won't go in the sandbag."
I Corps Tactical Zone

2.3 *Operation Apache*

Operation Apache: friendly fire, June 12, 1966.

During the first part of June, Fox Company went on a search and destroy mission, code named Apache, which consisted of two reinforced companies, Fox Company and Echo Company. They were to execute a Heliborne assault into a LZ in the Quan Ly Tin area.

Upon the completion of the Helo assault, they established a combat base and conducted a search and destroy operation in the assigned tactical area. Fox Company landed at LZ Cobra where they immediately encountered light enemy contact from long range sniper fire. Two batteries of 105 mm Howitzers was heli-lifted into the LZ; the first time a battery was heli-lifted in support of the Second Battalion in Vietnam.

During the next couple days, light contact was made with the Viet Cong. Finally, on the last day, Fox Company was to sweep towards the battalion command post and be heli-lifted to Hill 69, but their plan was halted as they came under sniper fire once again.

Hank Januchowski (Ski) was on the trail about 20 yards in front of Barnes and the machine gunner was about 20 yards behind Barnes. Word was passed down the line that artillery had been called in on the enemy to our front. Barnes had noticed a trench line that had been dug about 25 feet to his right along the trail and quickly took a kneeling position when rounds began whistling over his head. The artillery battery was positioned to their rear which meant the artillery had to be called over their position in order to strike the enemy. Barnes knew this was not the ideal scenario due to the possibility of a short round. The first three rounds came whistling directly overhead and as the fourth round came, Barnes heard silence, followed by a sudden explosion. He was blown into the air with his helmet following close behind. His ears were ringing as he lay on the ground; the air around him filled with smoke. Shaking the dirt from his body, he managed to get back up into a standing position, his head throbbing. As he looked around to all the trees and vegetation that had been split in every direction from the blast, he realized the 105 Howitzer round had fallen squarely into the trench line, 25 feet to his right. If it had landed anywhere else, he wouldn't have survived. The depth of the trench had deflected the shrapnel at a 45° angle, just above his head; fate spared his life by inches.

2.4 *Supply Routes & Nightly Ambushes*

October 1, 1966

Fox Company along with Hotel Company and Golf Company moved north from Chu Lai to Dong Ha while Echo Company stayed on the perimeter of Hill 69 in Chu Lai. The Third Battalion, Fifth Marines had been operating out of that area for some time. Three companies of the Second Battalion moved north to assist the Third Battalion in kicking off Operation Prairie.

Things would change for Fox Company during the beginning of October 1966. The battalion's move to Dong Ha put the company right in the middle of the 324-B Division of the North Vietnamese Army. The 324 Division consisted of somewhere between 8,000 to 10,000 soldiers, with plenty of weapons and supplies.

Prior to Fox Company's arrival, September had consisted of heavy fighting and enemy contact during Operation Hastings, an attempt to push the 324 Division north, back across the DMZ (Demilitarized Zone). However, the operation failed and the North Vietnamese Army was still operating with heavy military numbers in the area.

October started with daily patrols and constant, nightly ambushes. Fox Company moved in and out of Dong Ha on mostly company size movements, meaning, we only had one company with us. Contact with the enemy only increased over time and casualties among Fox Company began to mount, reinforcing the deadly statistic of a 50% death rate associated with the Fifth Marines. On almost every patrol, the Marines would find abandoned positions and equipment consisting of: packs, ponchos, bags of rice, bottles of medicine, uniforms, empty 82 mm mortar canisters and deserted documents.

Barnes, Januchowski & Osborne: Operation Prairie

Osborne digging a machine gun position for the night

On October 8, elephant tracks along a heavily used trail—
what was believed to be a supply route—were discovered.

On October 9, Fox Company patrol found another trail of fresh elephant tracks at different coordinates from the first. The North Vietnamese Army was using elephants to carry supplies down from the north to resupply their armies in the south. For the next couple of days, Fox Company along with Hotel Company, made heavy contact with the enemy on numerous occasions, with Marines being killed or wounded on every engagement.

On October 15, Fox and Golf Company performed a two company sweep. At 1305 hrs, Marines from Fox Company discovered one, armed Viet Cong and attempted to apprehend the soldier. As he fled, the Marines were unable to capture him; he would have to be shot. At the same time, the Second Platoon was under sniper fire from two other enemy soldiers. The Marines returned fire and while searching the area, Barnes and two other Marines located one of the snipers hiding in a village hamlet. While two of the Marines attempted to hold the soldier down, Barnes pulled out a machete from his pack. He walked over to a bamboo pole alongside the hamlet door that had a piece of cord tied around the center, with the intention of using the cord to tie up the enemy soldier, but as he approached with his machete, the North Vietnamese soldier took one look at him and frantically began to struggle against his captors. He began biting their arms and managed to jump up from the ground and run towards a thicket of bamboo. Barnes fired one shot, killing the enemy soldier in an instant. As they continued their search, two packs, four grenades, and a Chinese made SKS rifle were found.

During this sweep, a French born photojournalist, Catherine Leroy, was assigned to Fox Company. She was working with Larry Burrows and Life Magazine on a story about the Fifth Marines in Vietnam. Catherine and Larry photographed Fox Company, Second Platoon for a short period of time during Operation Prairie while Corporal Barnes and Januchowski along with his gun team, provided security.

42

SGT Hank Januchowski and L/CPL Richard Sauerman

L/CPL John Wilson, 3.5 rockets crossing River South of the DMZ

Second Platoon on sweep, South of the DMZ

2.5 *The First Loss*

Barnes loses his first machine gunner, October 26, 1966.

There were no misses on a battlefield, a bullet either wanted you or it didn't.

As a Marine in 2/5, you trained together as a unit in every capacity while in Okinawa. You went through the northern training, guerrilla warfare school together and this created a sense of pride; it created a sense of comradery, fellowship and loyalty called, *esprit de corps*. After the first couple of months, the constant shuffle of Marines between units began to break that sense of team spirit. The logic behind spreading out the combat-experienced Marines, a majority of which were volunteers to first hit the shores of Vietnam, amongst the draftees, who were fresh out of boot camp, was understandable. However, the Marines began to witness a change in attitude. They were always willing to maintain a sense of readiness for battle, but it became apparent that there was a loss of that well-cultivated, "gung-ho" spirit.

The Marines faced an array of problems during those early months in Vietnam. The companies were starting to notice a lack of experienced Sergeants and NCOs (Non-Commissioned Officers) holding positions and instead, they were being filled by lower ranking, non-commissioned officers than what the billet within the company called for. This would be mentioned many times in the battalion's monthly operational logs. It especially held true moving into the latter part of 1966 and early 1967.

Towards the end of 1966 through mid 1967, Barnes held a rank at least two pay grades below what his job description called for in the weapons platoon. Rank in combat during the Vietnam War could not come fast enough for the need within the battalion. The Marine Corps had long since done away with combat promotions. I believe, to this day, there would have been better cohesion within the units if this had not been done. Marines usually accepted and respected rank over position.

At the end of September 1966, 2/5 moved their tactical area of operation and the command post from Hill 69 in Chu Lai to Dong Ha. From that area of operation, Fox Company started a series of aggressive patrols and ambushes. The company continued to have a critical shortage of Officers and NCOs.

October 9, 1966, Fox Company embarked on Operation Prairie. This operation would be a reconnaissance in force. Shortly after Operation Prairie on October 26, Fox Company was headed back to base camp at Dong Ha in a company size force. On its return, Barnes lost his first machine gunner on his gun team.

When a Marine company moved from one location to another, the typical column formation was: one machine gun team to the rear of the column and one machine gun team to the front of the column. The lead gun team was usually right behind the point man. The point man being the Marine who was assigned to walk on point in the front of the column. This was probably one of the most dangerous positions in a moving formation. On that morning, Barnes' machine gun team was directly behind the point man, to the front of the column. Behind the point man was the machine gun squad leader Corporal Hank "Ski" Januchowski, who was a close friend to Barnes and would stay that way until he rotated back to the states in May 1967. Behind Corporal Januchowski was Rick "Hawkeye" or "Barney" Barnes. It seemed every Marine in Vietnam carried a nickname including the company itself. The nickname for our company at the time was "Burgett's Bastards," named after our Company Commander, Captain George Burgett. Behind Barnes was Norm "Ozzie" Osborne, his machine gunner.

The column moved down a trail near a small village, lined with a number of village *hooches* or huts where the families lived. As the column neared a section of the trail that was 100 meters before a sharp right turn, Barnes glanced over to the opening of one of the hooches. In the doorway stood a *mama san*—a name that referred to the head female of the household—and next to her on the right, was a young Vietnamese boy around six years old. To the left of the Vietnamese woman was a female girl about eight years old. As Barnes looked into her eyes, she shook her head to the left and right with no other expression on her face. Barnes knew something wasn't right. There were always American sympathizers in some of these villages, but you never knew who they sided with; trust was always a risk.

A few minutes earlier when they entered the village, Barnes recognized the smell; it was a scent that brought back vivid memories of the enemy fleeing into the jungle after entering a Viet Cong encampment, a smell he would never forget. Both American and North Vietnamese soldiers said they could smell their enemy before they saw them. Rick could smell the North Vietnamese before hearing them; the smell was not like yours or mine.

Barnes immediately turned to his rear, "Ozzie, remove your machine gun from your shoulder, something is about to happen." Barnes flipped the selector lever on his M-14 to fully automatic. He normally carried a 20-round magazine inserted in the rifle with another 20-round magazine taped upside down, attached to the inserted magazine. This gave him 40 rounds to his automatic disposal with the flip of his wrist.

He motioned to Januchowski at his front and advised, "Ski something is about to happen." Ski immediately went to his ready. Within moments, the point man turned at the right angle on the trail, Ski with Barnes' gun team followed directly behind.

Barnes glanced to his left and saw a dirt-covered mat pop open, just 15 feet away. From the spider trap came a burst of fire into his machine gunner Ozzie. Barnes immediately opened fire with his automatic into the Viet Cong. Before Barnes could hit the ground, he had flipped his second magazine and fired an additional 20 rounds into the soldier.

The ambush had been sprung and an immediate hail of bullets followed, ammunition whizzing by in every direction. As Barnes lay on the ground he could hear Ozzie hollering, "Barney I'm hit! Barney I am hit!" Barnes immediately jumped up from the ground and ran back towards Ozzie amidst a hail of gunfire. Throwing his M-14 rifle on Ozzie's chest, he grabbed Ozzie's machine gun. Ozzie had a 100-round bandolier connected and wrapped around the gun. With the machine gun now in Barnes' hands, he turned to the trench line that had been dug along the trail to his right. Seeing several enemy soldiers running along the trench, he fired the M-60 machine gun up and down their pathway. Barnes unsnapped another 100-round bandolier from around his chest and continued firing into the escaping soldiers.

Out of ammunition yet again, Barnes ran back to Ozzie's ammo humper, PFC Phil "Philly Dog" Hollins. Barnes grabbed another 100-round bandolier from Philly Dog and ran back into the village. It seemed that as quick as the ambush had started, it was over. Looking down at the machine gun, an enemy AK 47-round had gone through the butt stock of the machine gun, hitting the buffer and coming out the bottom of the stock. Whether the round came while Ozzie was carrying the gun or Barnes, one of them had skirted another round by mere inches.

By the time Barnes returned to Ozzie, he was being moved to a separate area where he was medevac'd with four other wounded Marines and one Marine KIA. After the ambush, the experience of surviving a barrage of bullets and coming out

unscathed, only increased the bond between Barnes and
Hank Januchowski.

Ozzie was medevac'd first to the *USS Enterprise* and then
transferred to the Medical Hospital ship, *The Repose*. Both
ships sat off the shore of Vietnam. While convalescing on *The
Repose*, Ozzie was visited by a four-star General.

Lewis Walt, the Marine Commanding General of the III
Amphibious Force, came to Ozzie's bedside to present him
with the Purple Heart. General Walt asked Ozzie, "Marine, is
there anything I can do for you?"

Ozzie said in reply, "Sir, can you get me a beer?" The Officer
standing next to the General looked at Ozzie in utter
bewilderment. The General walked away and after a few
minutes, returned with a beer in his hand, passing it to Ozzie.
Afterwards, the Marines in the hospital bunks around him
could not believe the General had returned with a beer,
much less that Ozzie had the nerve to ask for one.

L/CPL Ozzie holding an M-60 machine gun

After the ambush, the village was thoroughly searched. The Marines found evidence of a platoon-sized unit being camped out there prior to the attack. Numerous boxes of medical supplies were found in an underground tunnel shelter. The puzzling part of the discovery wasn't the supplies or the amount found, but rather, what they were labeled with; each box was stamped with "Berkeley California" in bold letters. This later caused a shit storm for the United States government and ultimately found its way back to the 2/5 Battalion Command.

It all stemmed from the letters that Barnes and Lance Corporal Donnie Fountain had sent home. L/CPL Fountain was a fire team leader in the Second Platoon, Foxtrot Company and was one of the Marines involved in the ambush as well as the search of the village afterwards. Barnes wrote a letter to his parents the day following the attack and shocking discovery, describing the events in detail.

Dear Mom, Dad & all,   October 27, 1966

How is everybody? Yesterday we got into a pretty bad firefight. Osborne, my gunner, was shot three times in the hip and leg. They hit us from trenches and spider traps as we moved through a village. I was right in front of Oz when he got hit. I shot the VC out of the spider trap that got him. We cleared the VC out of the village. When we searched that village, we found crates of medical supplies and blood sent to the VC from Berkeley California. It was stamped all over the boxes. I'm still alive but a lot of my buddies got shot up real bad. Most of the guys are writing and are going to try and get this published in every newspaper possible. It'll probably do no good, but the Marines in my unit especially, because we found our own proof and would like to know why we have to fight the VC and the Americans both. It was the same as those people from Berkeley shooting Oz and the rest of the guys yesterday. Those people in Berkeley and all the rest of them in the United States who are sending supplies here to the Viet Cong don't realize what they're doing because they don't have to watch their buddies die. I never realized what and how this war was until I came here 29 days ago to the DMZ where men die every day. I probably shouldn't have said all I did in this letter, but I want you to know just what's happening. We are clearing the VC out of the area, but they keep moving right back in. As long as we are here, we'll do our best to get this war over with. The greatest thing about the Marines and the guys I fight next to, we'll all die for our country. I must close for now. I will write as soon as possible

Love,
RICK

FIGHTING TWO ENEMIES

"All warfare is based on deception."
-Sun Tzu

3.1 *Aid to the Enemy*

Friday, November 18, 1966

Chicago Tribune headline reads:
AID TO VIET CONG STIRS STORM

Veteran groups in Chicago and throughout the nation were indignant yesterday about reports that medical supplies seized from fleeing communist troops in Vietnam carried labels reading Berkeley California. Giving the Viet Cong medicine is just as bad as giving them ammunition, said James Hayes, commander of the American Legion Cook County council. I am sure I speak for legionnaires and veterans everywhere when I say this is disgusting.

Marines fighting in Vietnam including one from Highland Indiana have written letters home describing the Berkeley medical supplies found after the capture of a Vietnamese village long held by the communist.

Last February 24th the campus progress of the labor party at the University of California in Berkeley announced that it had sent $1500 worth of medical aid to the Viet Cong. University officials said the group no longer exists.

"It is totally revolting that citizens of this country would send supplies to the enemy," said Leslie M. Fry, a Reno Nevada attorney who is National Commander of the Veterans of Foreign Wars. Fry and William R. Moran, State VFW Commander, urged Congress to pass laws to prevent Americans from sending aid to the communist.

"The time has come since there is no formal declaration of War for Congress to act to outlaw this type of thing," Fry said. He said the medical supplies are used to treat communist troops wounded in battle with Americans.

A somewhat different point of view was expressed by Elmer K Johnson, newly elected Commandant of the Chicago Marine Corps league, who suggested that the supplies may have been intended for American forces, but were stolen by black marketeers in Vietnam and sold to the communist.

Details on the medical supplies were contained in a letter from Lance Corporal Rick Barnes, 19, a machine gun team leader with Company F, Second Battalion, Fifth Marines, fighting in the former demilitarized zone between north and south Vietnam.

The Tribune carried a similar account yesterday from a Marine from Oklahoma. Corporal Barnes, in a letter to his parents, Mr. and Mrs. Charles E Barnes, of Highland, told of clearing the communist out of a village in a bloody battle on October 26 in which a friend was wounded. "In the village we found crates of medical supplies and blood plasma stamped Berkeley California," he wrote. "I don't know why we have to fight the VC and Americans both—It was the same as those people from Berkeley shooting Oz, his friend—those people don't realize what they're doing because they don't have to watch their buddies die."

Mrs. Tommy Fountain of Norman, Oklahoma, mother of the other Marine who had complained of finding the Berkeley labeled medical supplies, said she informed the Federal Bureau of Investigation and was told an investigation would be made. "Why would Americans help kill us?" Corporal Donnie Fountain told his mother, "There's only one name for Americans who give aid and comfort to their enemy, and that's *traitor*."

In a Norman Oklahoma newspaper, Lance Corporal Fountain's Family gave the paper the following account:

He sat in the moonlight after he had seen his friends die, an Oklahoma boy far from home, and he wrote a letter to his folks:

Dear Mom and Dad,

I ask only one thing of you at this time (wrote Donnie Ray Fountain, 20 years old, of the First Marines) and that is for you to see this letter gets to the papers.

His parents Mr. and Mrs. Tommy fountain of Norman Oklahoma made sure the letter got to the transcript.

"If I could have only one wish now," the Marine had written, "it would be that everyone in America could have seen what we all saw yesterday."

While on a company size patrol we entered the village returning to our base camp. Our platoon was moving through when we were ambushed from auto weapon fire on our right flank.

I saw four of my buddies cut down by fire. We killed eight and wounded no telling how many. Every fighting man in Vietnam knows and believes his cause for fighting is worth it and he is willing to give his all. There's not one thing these people demonstrators can do to stop us from fighting for a free way of life, either.

We've been called everything from murderers to baby killers, are we the murderers?

There's only one name for Americans who give help and comfort to the enemy, traitors. Don't worry about me, I have all my faith in God. I am well and doing fine. I just couldn't sleep till I had written this to let you know how I feel. I'll try and write to you for a long time tomorrow. Take care of yourself and please keep your prayers coming.

Your loving son,
Donnie

During the second week of December 1966, Staff Sergeant Sprimont walked up to Corporal Barnes with a concerned look, "Barnes, the Battalion Commander, Lieutenant Colonel Airhart, wants to see you at his command post."

"Captain Burgett wants to see me?" asked Barnes.

"No Barnes, the Battalion Commander. It can't be good so put on some clean jungle fatigues and clean yourself up. I have no idea what he wants."

For just an instant Barnes thought, it certainly isn't for a battlefield commission, they stopped doing that years ago. What could it possibly be for? Barnes truly had no idea why he had been ordered before the Battalion Commander.

Wasting no time, Barnes appeared at the doorway of the battalion command post. He entered and stood before the Colonel's Command Desk at attention.

Lieutenant Colonel Airhart addressed Barnes in an angered tone, "Corporal Barnes, you have caused a shit storm and I am pissed off. I have the news, media, congressmen, and the upper echelon down my ass. All because you and Corporal Fountain decided to write letters home to Mom and Dad. You both know that when you are in country, in combat situations, you do not write home *anything* that happens under this battalion's command. Furthermore, if anything like this happens again, you will be standing before something very larger than I am. Corporal Barnes, get your ass back to your Company and keep your mouth shut."

As he walked back to the Fox Company's staging area, Barnes thought of the pride he had acquired since he had enlisted in the Marine Corps. He felt a tremendous amount of self-worth and fulfillment from being a Marine; fighting alongside his brothers in Vietnam formed a bond that could never be broken. He was living and fighting with guys that he would lay down his life for and he knew they would do the same. Barnes recalled a phrase he had heard during his first few months in Vietnam when another Marines' actions had been questioned, the Marine laughed and said, "What are they going to do, send me to Vietnam?" With that reassurance, Barnes had a feeling that everything was going to be just fine. He had already been through the worst or so he thought.

3.2 *Con Tien*

November 1966

A recon mission was about to become the worst five days since arriving in Vietnam.

There was a specific area in Vietnam that was named The Hill of Angels or Hill 158 by the early missionaries that first arrived. Hill 158 was located only three miles from the demilitarized zone separating North and South Vietnam. The base, first created by the U.S. Army Special Forces in early 1966, later transitioned to operational control by the Marine Corps.

Fox Company moved into a portion of Hill 158 and immediately started establishing a command post by clearing and digging fox holes. A few months later, Hill 158 became known as Con Tien or as the Marines called it, Foxtrot Hill. The area enclosing the base was a thick jungle with distant hills, covered in heavy vegetation. It was said that the wind at this location made a sucking sound, as if those stationed inside were in a natural wind tunnel, rather than a breeze flowing through the air. Con Tien, along with the surrounding areas, was later known as Leatherneck Square, in honor of the Marines that would lose their lives there in the coming months.

Over the next month, numerous patrols and ambushes operated from the base the Marines had temporarily established as Foxtrot Hill. The company's move into the area was part of Operation Prairie and it was finally starting to resemble something functional; all supplies were flown in by helicopter including water, which was only enough for drinking purposes. By the time the company returned to An Hoa the first week of December, Barnes had gone 57 days without a shower. His jungle fatigues had quite literally started to rot off his body; the lack of hygiene had caused numerous problems throughout the company. Any cuts or injuries acquired, usually led to infections that only a strong antibiotic could clear it up. If not, evacuation by helicopter was required.

Another problem at the base was large Vietnamese centipedes. They were orange-red in color and were about 8-10 inches long. If bitten, they caused extreme pain and in rare cases death. They crawled into your fox hole at night or under your fatigue shirt while sleeping. The centipedes preferred a warm area, so it wasn't uncommon to wake up in your fox hole, roll over and either be bitten by a centipede or stung by a scorpion.

While there, the Marines made little contact on patrols or ambushes, it seemed the North Vietnamese Army was bypassing their position and moving further south. The buildup by the North Vietnamese Army was later found to be in the Que Son Valley.

Being only three miles from North Vietnam, there was a constant fear of the base being hit by North Vietnamese artillery. That threat fueled deeper fox holes, but because it was the beginning of monsoon season, the heavy rains turned them into muddy baths. Every morning the Marines used their helmet covers to empty water from their fox holes. On a positive note, the monsoons provided water for a futile attempt at showering. Unfortunately, it was maybe sufficient for the first 5-10 guys who quickly soaped up and hoped there was enough water to rinse off. Creativity was a necessary skill for jungle survival and the showering contraption was no exception. By building two sandbag walls, placing two bamboo poles that stretched from one wall to the other across the top, cutting a hole in the bottom of a 55-gallon drum for a faucet, and fashioning two ponchos above the drum to funnel rainwater, a makeshift shower was fashioned.

CPL Rick Barnes and CPL Januchowski attempting to stay dry during the monsoon season

It was during this time in Vietnam that Corporal Barnes and the rest of the company came in contact with the herbicide now known as Agent Orange. During the first week of setting up our defensive positions and perimeter, a team of Marines were flown in by helicopter. Using backpacks for spraying, they emptied numerous canisters of Agent Orange herbicide, covering the entire hill; within a week, the foliage was dead or dying. Fox Company continued digging their fox holes and setting up their perimeter. They slept and lived in the area sprayed with Agent Orange.

With the base camp being so close to the DMZ, Barnes often crossed over into North Vietnam while on patrols. Although not authorized, crossing was not uncommon. You knew when you had crossed the line because there was a clearing, wider than two football fields in length, as far as the eye could see with absolutely no foliage. On one of Barnes' patrols, he had crossed the opening and was about halfway when a large prop-driven military aircraft approached their patrol. The plane was following the cleared pathway. Their first thought was, is it ours or a North Vietnamese Army aircraft. It became evident that the aircraft was spraying the herbicide Agent Orange from large sprayers across the length of the wingspan and the patrol had nowhere to seek cover. As the engines roared overhead, Barnes could feel the dampness spread over his body and seep through his fatigues from the herbicide. Because hygiene was so bad at the camp, Agent Orange remained on their body for long periods of time.

As time progressed, long after the war, the severe implications of exposure to Agent Orange surfaced, leaving many Marines with deadly diseases and illnesses to battle.

After being at Con Tien for three weeks, a Marine from Second Platoon came down to the fox hole where Corporal Barnes had his gun team on the perimeter, "Barnes, the Gunny wants to see you."

Barnes immediately thought about the last time he got called in to see the Gunny and ended up in front of the Second Battalion Commander regarding the Berkeley medical supply debacle. He racked his brain for anything he had done that could have possibly violated regulations, but the only thing he could come up with was crossing the DMZ into North Vietnam a few times and he wasn't in charge on either of those patrols.

The only other thing it could be in reference to was an incident while on Hill 69. Before being sent further north, two

Australian recon soldiers came through the perimeter where Barnes' gun team was positioned. The two were the baddest looking soldiers he had seen since landing in Vietnam; they reeked of confidence and combat. They were hard-core, war-ready, make you shit-your-pants kind of G.I. Joe's with a necklace of "trophy ears" adorning their necks; the kind of guys you'd want next to you when facing the enemy. Their mementos were garnered from cutting off the enemy's ears after conquering them. They'd dry them out in the sun to the point where they resembled shriveled raisins and then thread them to wear around their neck. It didn't take long for an order to come down from the Battalion Headquarters: No trophy ears in Fox Company. Did they think he was part of that? He hadn't collected any trophy ears himself, but he could be guilty by association.

Barnes walked up to the company command post, still pondering the reason for being summoned. Gunny Jones addressed him promptly, "Barnes, you always seem to be the first gun team in front of a patrol or the last team protecting our rear. You always have your hand up when they ask for a volunteer gun team. I thought of you first. This is not an order, it's a volunteer mission. We've got a recon team on the hill. It's a five-man team but they lost their machine gunner a couple days ago. They need a gun. They've got an important recon mission. There is supposed to be a large movement of the North Vietnamese Army, maybe battalion size, moving a few miles northeast of our position. They want to get an exact location and drop some artillery and airstrikes on top of them before they get here. Are you interested? They only need one man with a gun."

Without even thinking it through and being logical, Barnes quickly responded, "Sure Gunny when do I leave?"

"Barnes you're only going to be gone a couple days and they travel light. No flak jacket, no pack, carry as many bandoliers as you can and still move fast." As Gunny Jones turned and threw him a soft boonie hat he added, "Oh, yes Barnes and no helmet. If you're going to run with them, you have to look like them and check in with me as soon as you get back."

As Barnes walked back to his gun team, he thought to himself, *what the fuck have I done.*

The First Force Recon (Long Range Reconnaissance Patrols)— some of the baddest, s.o.b's in the war—were units of four or six Marines who played cat-and-mouse with the enemy to try and figure out their positions. They operated in places everyone else was afraid to go. If you saw them in a civilized setting, they were likely to be drunk and abusive.

Back at his gun team position, Barnes let his machine gunner, Gary "Astro" Asbell, know what he had volunteered for. He grabbed the M-60, making sure he had a full 100 round bandolier already wrapped around the gun. He then grabbed three more 100 round bandoliers crisscrossing them across his body. This gave him 400 rounds at his disposal. Barnes then took a couple cans of c-rations and stuck them in his fatigue pants side pocket. Making sure he had two full canteens, he picked up an empty c-ration can and clipped it in where the ammo pouch is normally attached on the side of the machine gun. When Barnes was a gunner he attached the c-ration can so the bandolier would feed into the gun more smoothly, preventing a possible jammed feed.

Quickly reviewing with his gun team what he had just volunteered for, he told Astro to give him his 45 pistol and traded him his M-14. Both Astro and Philly Dog thought he had gone nuts. After strapping on his K-bar knife, Barnes turned to Astro and said, "Tell Ski when you see him, I will see him in Chi Town or on the flipside."

"Chi Town?" Astro asked.

"He'll know what I mean."

Both Barnes and Januchowski were from Chicago and had become very close since fighting alongside one another in Vietnam for several months. They had bonded like brothers.

Barnes moved on down to the perimeter where the rest of the team was waiting for him at the wire. All five Marines looked at him as though they were sizing him up; probably wondering if he was up to what might lie ahead. All they said to Barnes before leaving was, "Stay close, don't lose us and keep your eyes open." They didn't even take the time to introduce themselves. But it was probably for the best, he didn't want to get too close, most were not likely to return anyway. Hopefully it was one day out and one day back.

After leaving the perimeter, they quickly moved into the heavy jungle foliage and further into the canopies. Barnes knew the importance of not being spotted by the enemy leaving the perimeter or entering the jungle. He thought back to how many patrols and ambushes he had been on, always company, platoon or at least squad size; never had he gone into no man's land, a.k.a. Indian territory, with only six men. Every scenario and problem they could run into starting flashing through his thoughts.

They moved fast, staying off the trails, out of open areas and keeping close to one another. When they left, it was late afternoon and within a couple hours Barnes was in a heavy, jungle canopy, unable to see the sky above. The team moved fast but careful, every Marine with his head on a swivel. All Barnes kept thinking was, North Vietnamese Army, battalion size...he wanted to find them, but not run into them.

Within a few hours, night started to set in. The team found a position under the jungle canopy that still gave a field of vision but afforded them plenty of concealment. When anyone spoke, they whispered. One of the Marines turned to Barnes and told him what his two-hour watch time was. He stated two men will be awake on each watch, absolutely no one fires a shot unless death is in your face. We cannot be detected. He didn't have to explain the seriousness of that statement any further. Barnes had been in Vietnam long enough to realize the importance of not being seen or heard.

Barnes quietly opened his first can of c-rations and ate the small portion of beef steak. One of the Marines turned to him and whispered, "When you're finished, keep the can or bury it." Barnes didn't ask, he already knew why. Leave no signs behind.

Barnes was awake at first light. One of the Marines that appeared to be in charge motioned for them to move out. They continued to move throughout the morning into the thick jungle canopy. Barnes could see the lead Marine occasionally stopping to check his map and compass. They continued throughout the day until midafternoon, when they stopped.

One of the Marines was carrying what appeared to be a PRC-25 Radio. Barnes could see three of them standing together talking. He heard one of them say he couldn't get the radio to work. Knowing very little about radios, Barnes had no idea if it was the battery or the lack of reception, all he knew was everyone seemed to be very concerned.

They moved through the heavy jungle until late afternoon, searching for another location to sleep for the night. Barnes was told what time his watch would be. It was still evident they had no communication with the outside world; the radio was not working. With no communication, if contact was made with the enemy, they would be on their own; no emergency evacuation would be made. Barnes' only decision for that night was, does he eat his last can of c-rations or hope for the best and preserve it in case they survive.

On the third morning, they woke up and continued to move. Barnes could see they were lost and still had no communication through the radio. With a heavy jungle canopy over their heads, there was no way of triangulating their location with the map. Barnes was starting to become very concerned and it was evident that the rest of the Marines felt the same way. They all knew that unless we could establish communication or walk themselves out of the thick jungle canopy, survival was becoming questionable.

The morning of the fourth day Barnes ate his last can of c-rations; water from his two canteens had been depleted the day prior. At this point, it seemed they were walking in circles. He didn't have the compass so he had no idea what direction they were going.

They sat in a night position on what seemed to be an extremely steep side of the mountain. By evening, Barnes started to wonder if they were ever going to get out of the jungle. He had long since questioned his decision to volunteer with Marines he didn't know, much less had never fought alongside.

This night, like every night in the jungle, was so still you could hear a pin drop. At 1400 hours, Barnes was awakened for his watch. Both he and the Marine next to him leaned back on the slope of the mountain side about six feet apart, listening for any sound in the dark of the night. Both Barnes and the Marine, after only 30 minutes into their watch, heard a rustling sound. It was coming from a location 30 to 40 feet in front of their position. It was clear their position had been compromised and they were being probed by the enemy to their front. They awakened the Marines on both sides of them. All Barnes kept thinking was what the one Marine had said the first night. Do not fire a single round until you see death in your face. All six Marines lay on the slope of the mountain, anxiously waiting for the enemy to be close enough to shoot.

As the rustling in front of them seemed to get within ten feet of their position, it suddenly broke at a full blast between Barnes and the Marine next to him. It immediately passed by his side, knocking him two or three feet to his left. Barnes realized it was a very large, wild boar.

All six Marines immediately breathed a sigh of relief. They were glad no one had fired a shot and their position had not been compromised.

As the morning sun began to rise on the fifth day, the six Marines got up from their night positions. They were all out of both food and water. Nobody had anything to drink for the last two days; food had been gone for three days. It was becoming evident both physically and mentally things were going to get worse, a lot worse, if they didn't get out of this jungle.

Not more than two hours later, at around 0800 hours, the six Marines, on a long since abandoned recon mission, walked into a clearing on the hillside, finally seeing the open sky.

The Marine towards the front spent ten minutes looking at the map then repositioning his compass until finally he pointed at an area one mile away, stating it was the fire base at Gio Linh; that's where we were going.

By early afternoon we arrived at the perimeter to the fire base, hacking our way through the jungle some 15 km (9 Miles) from Con Tien to Gio Linh. Five days after leaving the perimeter at Con Tien, four Marines stood by a bunker inside the perimeter at Gio Linh. Two of the Marines went to the base command post. Only 45 minutes later, the two returned and told him, pointing to a UH-34 helicopter sitting on an LZ some 200 yards away, "The pilot in that chopper has agreed to drop you off at Con Tien on his way back."

"Good luck guys. I thought I had a dangerous MOS...I will stay in Fox Company, you guys can keep your job." Barnes said, while shaking hands with all five Marines before walking away.

As the helicopter pulled away from the Gio Linh firebase, Barnes sat in the doorway of the helicopter alongside the door machine gunner. He looked out over the tops of the jungle canopies and at the Marine sitting behind his M-60 machine gun, his own M-60 straddled across his lap, and thought to himself, the door gunners' job is the one he wanted. He would rather be on top of these jungle canopies than underneath them. The last five days had been the worst five days since arriving in Vietnam eight months ago.

As the helicopter touched down on the Con Tien combat base, Barnes nodded to the door Gunner as he jumped onto the ground.

Walking up to the Fox Company command bunker, he could see Gunny Jones standing next to the entrance, "Barnes, son-of-a-bitch, I wrote you off dead—two days ago. Where the fuck have you been!?"

"Gunny, before I get into the last five days, one thing I would like to make clear sir, this is the last recon mission I will ever volunteer for." Barnes often wondered if any of those five recon Marines lived to make it home.

3.3 *The Build Up*

December 1966

Build up in the Que Son Valley—evidence of what lies ahead.

During the month of December, Fox Company would again operate out of the An Hoa Combat Base. Their operational control would move from the ninth Marine Regiment back to the First Marine Division. It would take Fox Company the entire month to adjust to its new tactical area of responsibility.

Aggressive patrolling, search and destroy operations were conducted every day in all areas of responsibility. Contact was almost a daily occurrence with constant pressure being brought against the Viet Cong.

The start of monsoon season caused constant problems for all operations. Roads became impassable with even the smallest streams swollen and, on several occasions, tactical units were unable to link up or close with the enemy because of the overflowing rivers and streams. Helicopter resupply of ammunition and rations as well as casualty evacuations were most difficult due to the low visibility and constant rain. Immersion foot or trench foot, an injury of the feet resulting from prolonged exposure to wet conditions, became a constant problem.

Another novelty Fox Company faced outside of actual combat, was the constant devastation caused by the ingenious, but deadly booby traps and mines. The mines were often made from unexploded bombs harvested after American bombing missions or American grenades lost in combat. The booby traps were an entirely different ball game. There was not one second to relax, the body was in a constant state of vigilance; looking out for bamboo and wooden spike traps that were intended to skewer their unsuspecting victims or hidden pits with spikes lying at the bottom, concealed by rice paddies. Everything and anything was used in order to injure or maim American soldiers, even bear traps or other animal traps. Marines in the field would become paranoid and the Commanders frustrated.

It became obvious there was a large number of North Vietnamese Army troops in the area.

At one point, in early December, some 600 Vietnamese civilians were evacuating in a column from the area. As the column proceeded through, more civilians would join; the young, old and sick all had to be evacuated by helicopter if available. The villagers from three hamlets in the area wanted to be evacuated, they were afraid of the Viet Cong. They said the North Vietnamese Army has control of the valley and has for the last two years. Evacuation from the valley would increase throughout the month to approximately 2,000 with the majority going out on foot.

This would only prove to be evidence of what was in store for the Marines in the Que Son Valley.

Hanoi Hannah

"Tokyo Rose" was a name given by allied troops fighting in the South Pacific during WW II to all female, English-speaking, radio broadcasters of Japanese propaganda.

There was one radio personality in particular, Trinh Thi Ngo or Thu Huonh (the GI's referred to as Hanoi Hannah), who maintained three, 30-minute segments of daily broadcasting on the network. Her scripts were written by the North Vietnamese Defense Ministry in an attempt to degrade US troops and convince them their cause was unjust. However, it had little effect on the troops and was seen more as entertaining than anything else.

Hanoi Hannah had a so-called "wanted dead or alive" list of US military units, in which Fox Company was mentioned frequently. The Marines in Fox Company considered it to be a "badge of honor" to appear in their propaganda so often.

3.4 *A Second Blow*

November 27, 1966.

Barnes loses his second machine gunner.

On November 27, 1966, Fox Company and the rest of Second Battalion would start their move from the Dong Ha Combat Base further north to An Hoa where the Second Battalion, Fifth Marines would set up their new command.

The An Hoa Combat Base was in the Que Son Valley which was located along the border of the Quang Nam and Quang Tin Provinces. During the Vietnam War, it lay in the southern part of South Vietnam's I Corps Military region. The area around Que Son Valley, covering approximately 20x20 miles, was surrounded by mountains. The entire valley was the Tactical Area of Responsibility (TAOR) for the Second Battalion. The northern border was the Song Ky Lam River which flowed east to the South China Sea. A supply line from Danang to An Hoa cuts across the river at Liberty Bridge near the Phu Loc 6 Outpost. Antenna Valley formed the southern border. The western border contained the Song Tu River separating 2/5's TAOR from the Arizona Territory to the north. The southern portion of that border crossed the Song Tu River and included the Nong Son Coal Mines Outpost.

Aerial view of An Hoa Combat Base

Aerial view of Fox Company, An Hoa Combat Base

Populous and rice rich, the valley was viewed as one of the keys to controlling South Vietnam's five northern provinces by the communists. By early 1967, at least two Regiments of the Second Division of the People's Army of Vietnam had been infiltrated into the area. The Que Son Valley was also recognized as strategically important by the US Military Assistance Command, Vietnam.

The move to An Hoa would totally change the type of combat for Corporal Barnes and the Marines of Fox Company. The enemy would change from mainly local force guerrillas to freshly trained North Vietnamese Army (NVA) troops moving down from North Vietnam and crossing the DMZ (Demilitarized zone).

Throughout 1966 and 1967 both the United States and North Vietnam steadily expanded their commitment to the war. US forces maintained an illusionary thought, that eventually American troops would kill off so many enemy soldiers that North Vietnam would no longer be able to replenish their numbers on the battlefield in the south. The Marines fighting in the mountains and rice paddies never understood or worried about the "strategy," all they knew was the rice paddies and villages were infested with booby traps, landmines and the North Vietnamese Army.

As the Commander-in-Chief of the communist military forces, Vo Nguyen Giap often remarked, American military forces were superior to his own by virtually every measure, but the Americans strategic assessment of the nature of the war, of their own strengths and weaknesses and those of their adversaries, were markedly inferior to those of the Hanoi and the southern insurgency.

The communist forces meant to inflict sufficient casualties on the Americans to undermine the Army's morale and most importantly, dissolve any support for the war at home.

Throughout the month of December, Fox Company would participate in numerous aggressive combat patrols and ambushes. The three companies of the Second Battalion rotated between An Hoa Base perimeter security, Phu Loc 6 and the Nong Son coal mines. The Marines conducted security for mine sweeps on the truck route from An Hoa to Phu Loc. Night ambushes, listening posts and day patrols would be conducted from all three locations.

Lance Corporal Jerald "Jerry" Westphal, was one of the married, squad team leaders in the Second Platoon. Jerry seemed to get more packages from home than any other Marine in the company—cookies, candy and more cookies. Sharing with his brothers in the platoon was a ritual; everyone gathered around when the mail chopper arrived because everyone knew that even if they didn't receive something, Westphal was getting a goody box.

Jerry had a battery powered record player like many of the Marines. Music was an important escape for the soldiers in Vietnam. Many iconic songs came out of the war such as:

"We Gotta Get Out of This Place"
"Nowhere to Run"
"Leaving on a Jet Plane"
"Chain of Fools"
"Purple Haze"
"Green, Green Grass of Home"
"Fortunate Son"

In the rear combat base at An Hoa, music was everywhere. Even on a patrol or a long march to an objective, when no one thought they could take another step due to exhaustion, someone would burst into song. It was a way to keep our morale up; a way to keep going. It was a sound from the "real world," a place we all wanted to get back to.

A few days before Christmas, Jerry got a three-foot tall, plastic tree from home. On Christmas Eve, the Marines of Second Platoon gathered around. We placed the tree on top of an ammo box, used shaving cream for snow and candles for lights; we had ourselves a Christmas tree. Jerry took a picture to send to his wife.

Over half the Marines in the picture did not live to see another Christmas, including Lance Corporal Jerry Westphal. Jerry died in the arms of Corporal Barnes on the battlefield of Union II. Every Christmas, Corporal Rick Barnes received a Christmas card from the Westphal family until they passed away a few years ago.

Corporal Barnes front left in picture.

Marines of Second Platoon with the Christmas tree

3.5 *Nong Son Coal Mines*

On December 30, 1966, Lieutenant Colonel Airhart selected Fox Company to conduct a search and destroy mission near the coal mines at Nong Son.

The battalion had expanded its TAOR to include as far south as the coal mines at Nong Son, which was located nine kilometers southwest of An Hoa Combat Base, and southwest to Antenna Valley. The Nong Son coal mines were situated directly across from the western edge of the Antenna Valley and were the only active mines in the country. No American force had operated in the vicinity of the mines until now.

Fox departed An Hoa at 0800. They were to replace a company of the Army of The Republic of Vietnam, ARVN, infantry at the Nong Son compound. The company marched for six hours east of the Song Thu Bon River from An Hoa. They arrived at a small hamlett at Khuong Thuong. The village was directly across from their objective the Nong Son coal mines. It was a rapidly flowing and torrential river from the heavy monsoon rains.

The decision was made to commandeer a number of sampans along the riverbank—small river crafts that sweep upwards on both ends—built by the village craftsmen. They were woven together with reeds and covered with a tar like substance. Each sampan could hold three or four Marines. To propel the boat, the operator at the rear would have to move the aft rudder to the left or right.

Crossing the river was more dangerous than it looked. The raging river tore at the boats, ruthlessly rocking them from side to side. Somehow, we managed to get the whole company across the river to the western side without anyone drowning.

Fox Company's Second and Third Platoons took over the bunkers, fortifying the small compound. The compound was constructed at the bottom of a long terrain finger that ran to the top of the nearly 300-meter hill, overlooking the river. It had French-built houses, some with generators, that were occupied by the multinational engineers working the mines. The First Platoon was sent up to secure the top of the hill.

Fox ran a few short patrols from the compound, but stayed close due to the constant heavy monsoon rains and the nonexistent resupply.

The local populace kept the Marines fed through the New Year's holiday with cooked rice, peppers, French bread and fruit.

On the afternoon of December 31, 1966, Corporal Barnes went with a squad-sized patrol outside the compound. On the return, the patrol passed through the housing area for the multinational workers. Along one of the streets there were various, open-air, street vendors set up. For the first time in the last nine months since being in-county, he saw a sign that read, *Hamburgers $1.00*. Stopping to consider the possibility, he looked around, noticing there were no cats or dogs in sight. Then pondering further, he realized he had never seen a cow during his entire time in Vietnam either...he decided against the hamburger. Instead, he purchased as many "Ba mui ba" rice beers as his gun team and himself could stash in their fatigue pockets along with a couple bottles of rice whisky, locally made, containing no label.

On his return, he managed to stay out of sight from the watchful eyes of the Officers and Staff NCO's. Rick Barnes and his gun team, along with the surrounding bunkers, brought in the New Year's celebration that year with plenty of hooch for all. Not sure what was in the whisky, but it sure did the job. Everyone could still see the next morning and no one suffered from alcohol blindness. Later, it was discovered that the hooch was a potent form of rice alcohol, infused with herbs, spices and wild reptiles like snakes, geckos and turtles.

Barnes with Wheeler and Giebus in front of French Arvin Compound at the Nong Son Coal Mines

Second Platoon Fox, New Year's Eve at Arvin Compound at Nong Son Coal Mines

Rick Barnes zoomed in, center

Shortly after New Year's, on January 5, 1967, Fox Company left the coal mines and participated in Operation Lincoln with Lieutenant Colonel Airhart's Command Group and Golf Company. The operation was intended to flush out the enemy from Antenna Valley. This would give Fox Company and the Second Battalion more freedom to operate in the valley.

January 6, 1967, at approximately 0945, on the second day of Operation Lincoln, Fox Company was moving east to link up with Golf Company.

Corporal Barnes' machine gun team was bringing up the rear of the column. After the earlier loss in October of Barnes machine gunner Ozzie, his gunner had been replaced by Private First Class Esquivel. When Ozzie was shot, Corporal Hank Januchowski was walking in front of Barnes' gun team. And ever since, Januchowski was never far from that position. It had become an understanding within the machine gun teams that if you wanted to find squad leader Corporal Hank Januchowski, just find Barnes. The two Marines had become like brothers, they knew how the other was thinking and what the other would do next in a combat situation; they had become dependent on having each other nearby.

PFC Esquivel was a hard charging Marine. In a very short time Barnes had become relatively close to Esquivel as well. The two Marines even joked that after the war they might become mercenaries and fight in other countries, coining the name, *Esquivel's Raiders*.

The majority of Fox Company had already crossed a tall four-foot-high rice paddy dike with two feet of water on each side. The heavy monsoon rains, which had been on and off for most of the morning, had filled the rice paddies to an exceptionally high level.

Bordering the north side of the rice paddy, approximately 300 yards, was a scattering of Vietnamese hooches with heavy trees and vegetation. The village was set on a hill with a slight incline.

Walking along the dike approximately 100 yards from the end, Corporal Januchowski was towards the front of Barnes while Esquivel was at his back.

Before reaching the end of the dike, a shot rang out. Corporal Barnes turned and saw PFC Esquivel flying off the dike, into the rice paddy. Jumping into the paddy, Barnes saw that Esquivel had been shot through the right wrist. The round must have been from a high-powered caliber sniper rifle because his hand was barely hanging from his arm, attached by only a few strands of muscle and flesh. Barnes pulled Esquivel up against the rice paddy where Esquivel was protected due to the height of the dike.

Alongside Esquivel was a small tree approximately 6 inches in diameter. This tree appeared to be the only tree along that dike and the only one in that entire rice paddy. Barnes stood to see if he could tell where the round had come from. He positioned his body square with the tree. Instantly, the second round rang out. The tree in front of Barnes' head immediately shattered in front of his face, just thick enough to stop the round from impacting his head.

He could see that the round had come from the village area. He then lowered further down behind the dike and pulled a bandage from his web gear. He attempted to wrap the bandage around Esquivel's hand and up around his forearm to keep the hand from falling off the arm.

During the time that Barnes was putting the bandage on Esquivel, Corporal Januchowski had grabbed Esquivel's machine gun and began firing in the area he estimated the sniper was located. Within a couple minutes, Staff Sergeant Sprimont came running back along the dike. He stopped within 20 feet of Barnes and Esquivel, hollering to Barnes, "Get your goddamn men and get across this dike!"

Barnes hollered back at Sprimont, "Sarge, there's a sniper with a high-powered rifle that has us zeroed in. I've got a wounded man shot up bad, you've got to get off the dike."

No sooner did those words come out of Barnes' mouth when the third round exploded into Staff Sergeant Sprimont's arm and side. His body flew at least 25 feet off the dike from the impact of the round. He landed in the water-filled paddy, his body pulsing, uncontrollably thrashing, as if his body had a spastic mind of its own.

It was only a short time before PJ Jones moved his gun team along the paddy behind the dike and maintained suppressive fire into the village. A couple of other Marines ran back along the dike, jumped off with a poncho and placed Staff Sergeant Sprimont's limp body onto the poncho. The two Marines then carried Sprimont to the other side of the paddy and onto solid ground. Corporal Barnes and his ammo humper were able to pull Esquivel back onto the dike and onto the ground as well. While this was happening, Corporal Januchowski, with Esquivel's machine gun, and PJ Jones with his machine gun, were able to maintain cover fire until all Marines had cleared the dike.

A short time later, when the weather had started to clear, we were able to get a medevac chopper to retrieve Staff Sergeant Sprimont and PFC Esquivel for medical attention; both were still alive when loaded onto the chopper.

One year later, Corporal Barnes would run into staff Sergeant Sprimont at the Camp Pendleton Hospital in California. Both Marines had been stationed there after Vietnam. Barnes was undergoing a third operation on his left arm from a combat wound sustained later in the war. Staff Sergeant Sprimont was still receiving medical care for his extensive injuries from that day in Vietnam.

A HINT OF HOPE

"Learn from yesterday, live for today, hope for tomorrow."

-Albert Einstein

4.1 _Do I Go or Do I Stay_

By mid-January, 1967, Corporal Barnes' tour of duty in Vietnam was coming close to a close.

Most Marines that served in a combat zone would rotate back to the states when their tour was out. Rotating and getting out of war was what they lived for, every day. When you got down to that last month you were a short timer. You counted the days, the hours, the minutes, even the seconds that you had left before you could return home.

Barnes would wake up every morning, sit on the edge of his fox hole or bunker, look up as if he's looking at God and say, "Thank you God for another day."

Barnes never worried about his back because he knew his brothers in Vietnam had him covered.

God gave him three brothers by birth, but when he got to Vietnam, God gave him a whole platoon of brothers.
We all grow up with a hero in our family. In Vietnam when the nights were dark and you knew your future was in doubt, the only thing you were sure of was the courage of the man beside you. In Fox Company, we all marched towards the sound of the guns. Barnes knew that these brothers were a special breed of Americans and they were here, risking their lives to keep America free. For them and his country, he was not leaving. His experiences over the past nine months in combat had forged a bond that had no parallel; it had become a part of him.

Corporal Barnes went to Gunny Jones and requested an extension for his tour of duty to stay in Vietnam.

4.2 *Extension*

January 25, 1967

30 Day Leave: Tour Extension

Barnes' tour extension had been approved and he was on a flight headed out of Vietnam, on his way to Chicago, Illinois.

Along with a second tour came a 30 day leave to return home.

24 hours later, Barnes was landing at the O'Hare international airport. The flight had taken him directly from a war zone in Southeast Asia, 8400 miles with temperatures at 100°F, to the blizzard of 1967 and 20°F.

As the plane touched down on the runway, the pilot came on the intercom and announced, "Ladies and gentlemen, this is your lucky day, we are the last flight landing at this airport. An unexpected blizzard has blown into the Chicago area. The airport has now been shut down."

The snow had started at 5:00 AM in the morning on Thursday January 26, 1967, and Rick's flight landed at 11:00 AM. By noon, eight inches had already accumulated on the ground at O'Hare airport and Barnes was barely able to catch a taxi out. The driver agreed to go as far south towards Indiana as he could, but some of the roads and highways were already shutting down. Fortunately, Barnes was wearing his winter dress greens with his heavier green blouse. Heading down the Kennedy Expressway, the taxicab driver was able to get him as far south as Hyde Park. At that point, the expressway was totally shut down from snow drifts, stranded vehicles and semi's littering the roadside.

During the afternoon, snow was compiling at a rate of 2 inches per hour and the winds were up to 50 mph.

RICK BARNES

After leaving the taxi, Rick walked for another mile until he was able to flag down an 18-wheeler semi-truck. Truck drivers during that period were a special breed; they were always picking up hitchhikers or helping stranded motorists along the highway. Many were ex-military and had served in either World War II or the Korean War. Rick's father was a truck driver and had served in the army for five years during World War II, fighting in South Africa, Italy and during the final push into Germany. It was a different time in history; back when the roads were safe and people would not hesitate to help a fellow American. Unfortunately, times have changed drastically.

The snow was drifting and traffic had come to a standstill. Rick got out of one truck, walked a mile or two and flagged down another truck that was still moving. Most vehicles, at that point, were unable to move in the heavy snow and drifts. Numerous times one of the truck drivers would let Rick sit in his cab until he could warm up long enough to get out and continue walking. Rick wasn't surprised when trucks would stop and offer him a ride. Truckers were patriotic and it certainly helped being in uniform. It wouldn't be until about 3:00 AM on January 27, that Rick finally reached Highland, Indiana at interstate 80-94 and Kennedy Avenue.

The snowstorm of 67 was a full-blown blizzard out of the northeast with snow drifts up to 15 feet. 50,000 cars, buses and trucks were scattered along the streets and expressways, leaving many stranded for hours in their vehicles. It caused the greatest disruption in the city of Chicago since the Chicago Fire of 1871. Airports would not open until midnight the following Monday. The death toll in the Chicago region would reach 60. To this day, it remains the greatest snowstorm in Chicago history. Rick's arrival back to the states was not the best timing.

At 3:00 AM on Friday, Kennedy Avenue and Highland, Indiana was a ghost town. Rick walked down Kennedy

Avenue for a few hours until he finally arrived at his parent's home around 5:00 AM.

Rick hadn't told his parents or his high school sweetheart, now fiancé, Susann Goenenwein, that he was coming home. To Rick, Susann was the cutest little German girl in high school and he told her would marry her as soon as he returned from Vietnam. Rick was not due to rotate back stateside until sometime in March.

Knowing where his father hid the key for the back door, Rick walked into the house and headed to the staircase. As he looked up, he saw his father walking down the stairs, holding a German Luger pistol. The same pistol he had taken off a dead German Officer during World War II.

His father hollered out, "Dammit son! I almost shot you!"

His father usually always knew where his boys were at; he knew, or thought he knew, that two of his boys were in Vietnam, one was in the hospital, recuperating from back surgery and the fourth was in the bedroom next to his.

Rick married his high school sweetheart Susann Goenenwein on February 7, 1967.

Because of his unannounced return, they married in a small ceremony with a short honeymoon in downtown Chicago. His brother Bill, was his best man.

By February 24, he was back fighting the war in Vietnam.

Rick and Susann Barnes on some R & R in Hawaii

Rick and Susann on leave, getting married

4.3 *Return to Vietnam*

The emotional stress of combat.

When Corporal Barnes returned to Vietnam in March of 1967, he arrived at the US Marine fire support base, southwest of Da Nang.

Fox Company was providing security for the nearby Nong Son Coal Mines. Rick's Second Platoon was dug in at the bottom of the 200-meter-high mountain. First Platoon occupied the middle level and the Third Platoon occupied the mountaintop with M-40 recoilless Rifles and 4.2 inch mortars.

For the next 10 days, Fox Company spent their time improving the defensive positions at the Nong Son outpost. They constructed well-fortified fighting positions, communication, trenches and perimeter wire obstacles. Night patrols, ambushes and listening posts were conducted adjacent to and across the river from, the combat base.

It was evident upon Rick's return to Vietnam that the stress of patrols, ambushes and combat was taking its toll on the Second Platoon. Patrols and ambushes had become a way of life. The number of Marines killed and wounded on a daily basis was startling.

On March 10, 1967, PFC Mike Hernandez arrived in Vietnam aboard a troop transport ship. His arrival was similar to Corporal Barnes' arrival, departing the transport ship, boarding the landing craft, and heading into the shores of Chu Lai while singing the Marine Corps Hymn. Mike had felt they were reliving a page from Marine Corps history.

Mike's grandmother had immigrated to Texas in 1911 from Calientes, Mexico. His grandfather had immigrated from Chihuahua City, during Mexico's Revolution. Mike's mother's brother had been killed in France during World War II and her older sister's husband sacrificed his life during the same war, fighting in the Pacific Theater. Mike's dad and his brother both served in Europe and were wounded in combat. Mike enlisted as a proud second generation Mexican American, carrying on his family's tradition of serving their country.

It would not take long for PFC Hernandez to experience his first taste of combat. Corporal Barnes and the Second Platoon had rotated back to An Hoa perimeter duty. The Second Platoon had been assigned as the Sparrow Hawk reactionary platoon. Sparrow Hawk was great duty until a Marine unit got in trouble and needed help. They had barely settled in at the An Hoa Base when it was reported that a patrol unit was ambushed in a village and were under attack with casualty numbers climbing. The Second Platoon immediately boarded helicopters and headed into battle.

Corporal Barnes was aboard with PFC Mike Hernandez, who was about to experience his first taste of death. After landing, Corporal Eddie Roberts' squad along with Corporal Barnes' machine gun team went ahead in an attempt to reach the stranded Marines. It wasn't long before Barnes and Roberts' squad reached the pinned down Marines. The gunfight continued with one Marine KIA and several wounded.

Mike Hernandez, along with members of his squad, had stayed back to secure the landing zone (LZ) for the medevac chopper to land. After 30 minutes, the chopper landed and Mike prayed he wouldn't have to witness the dead and wounded being loaded on their way out. Unfortunately, Mike was in the evacuation line and lifting the Marines into the chopper, dead or alive, was part of the job. Mike wondered what the next 11 months would entail if he's already had to stare death in the face.

Mike reflected on his time aboard the troop transport ship coming to a foreign land. He had picked up a booklet on how to pray the rosary. Mike had responded to the rosary in group prayer ever since he had been able to speak. The rosary was said in church during the Lenten season and especially during funerals. From that day on, after seeing his first dead Marine, Mike began to call on prayer to get him through firefights, sniper fire and running through imminent danger to reach safety.

When under fire, he would feel a high pitch of anxiety. He ran across rice paddy dikes saying the Hail Mary or "Our Father" repeatedly. He saw many Marines killed and wounded every day, yet he was still standing. On many occasions he would see dirt flying up as rounds hit the ground nearby or hear the crack and snap overhead of a bullet impacting the tree branches above him. He was about to go on many company, platoon and squad size patrols and operations where he would see Marines die, wounded or medevac'd out; never knowing if any actually lived to see another day. The Marines never knew who was next. They often had no idea of the name of the operation or the purpose of the mission. All they knew was they were going to get up at 0-dark-hundred and prepare to jump off.

Every patrol or ambush that left the perimeter needed one of Barnes' machine gun teams.

On one such night, Barnes awakened his machine gunner, Astro. Astro looked up, "Barney, I'm not going, I quit."

"Astro you can't just quit, you will be court-martialed for disobeying a direct order."

Astro looked up at Barnes again and said, "I don't give a fuck Barney, I am telling you, I quit. I can't take it anymore."

Corporal Barnes spent the next 10 minutes convincing Astro to pick up his machine gun and go with him.

Astro must have had a premonition of what lay ahead. A week later, on March 17, while on a platoon size ambush, Gary Asbell would be shot and wounded while setting into another ambush site.

4.4 *Jammed Up*

March 1967

During the Vietnam war, well over 1 million American military soldiers would serve in combat in Vietnam. Nearly 48,000 American soldiers were killed by hostile fire. Well over 300,000 soldiers would be wounded, of which, 75,000 would be severely disabled.

In 1964, Defense Secretary Robert McNamara ended all procurement for the M-14 rifle. The M-14 was a product of the Army's arsenal system; the Army Materiel Command and the Ordinance Department, as it was called during the Vietnam War. The Ordinance Department was in charge of small arms development for the Army for more than 100 years. When the Vietnam War started, the M-14 rifle was the weapon of choice for both the Army and the Marine Corps. In 1964-1966, most military troops were being trained with the M-14 rifle for combat.

The M-14 rifle fired a 7.62 x 51 mm NATO cartridge designed for longer range accuracy. During the early part of the 1960s, Colt Manufacturing Company started developing and testing a new weapon called the M-16. The M-16 was a lighter weapon, firing the smaller 5.56 caliber rounds. The M-16 promised to be light weight and more lethal on the battlefield. The U.S. Army in 1965 and 1966 was the first US ground forces to begin Issuing the rifle to its troops in Vietnam. Despite the apprehension of the M-16 with its plastic parts replacing the all wood and steel M-14, the rifle would begin to stream into Vietnam in the summer of 1966.

Rumors of problems with the M-16 began to filter out of Vietnam. The rumors would include failing to feed, failing to fire and failing to extract. As The days and months continued, so did the complaints that were piling up. Commanding Officers of many of the troop commands in the Army reported the problems to their higher subordinates to the extent that confidence was degraded.

The harsh jungle climate corroded the rifle's chamber, exacerbated by the manufacturers decision against chrome plating the chamber. The ammunition that accompanied the rifles sent to Vietnam was incompatible with the M-16 and was the principal cause of the failure to extract malfunctions. During the early testing phase of the M-16, the ball powder made the rifle fire too fast and then jam.

The manufacturing company finally stated that it could no longer be responsible for the M-16's passing the Army's acceptance test; it could not guarantee performance with the ball powder.

Failure rate of the M-16 during firing was way above 50%. The Army's attitude was, you can use whatever ammunition you want for the test but we're going to keep sending the ball powder to Vietnam. Thousands of rifles were sent to Vietnam with the military being on notice that the rifles failed to meet design and performance specifications. The Army Assistant Secretary of Defense for Logistics knowingly accepted these M-16 rifles despite the fact they didn't pass the test. The failure by these officials within the Army to correct these deficiencies of the 5.56 mm ammunition bordered on criminal negligence. When they finally did go to Vietnam to inspect the weapons used by the troops, they blamed the problem on inadequate cleaning and maintenance of the rifles.

Nothing was being done to correct the problem until soldiers began writing home to their parents and girlfriends about the issue. They wrote about ambushes and battles where they would run into reinforced platoons of hard-core Viet Cong and when checking the bodies of their fallen comrades, they would find that a majority of their rifles had rounds stuck in the chambers. Soldiers would speak of having to use their cleaning rods to unjam the stuck rounds. After almost half the rounds they would fire, their cleaning rod would have to be used to eject the casing from the chamber.

They reported troops being overrun and the enemy taking the soldiers' equipment, but always leaving the M-16s behind; even the enemy knew our weapons were worthless. Several of those troops were found with their weapons dismantled, evidence that during the battle they had frantically attempted to correct the malfunction before being taken over. The weapon never manifested its true problems until there was heavy engagement with the enemy because it was during major engagements where rapid firing was necessary.

The Army continued to decline the chrome plating of the chamber and the rifle continued to suffer from corrosion problems. The rifle stock had a tendency to crack. The barrel and bolt carrier group and other steel parts would rust. The wrong ammunition continued to be shipped to the troops in the jungles. The brass ammunition casings were too soft, leading to ripped rims during the extraction process.

By 1967, Colt and the Army agreed to implement a number of modifications to the rifle to increase reliability. A heavier buffer would be installed to slow down the M-16 rate of fire. The plastic stock would be made more rugged by using thicker plastic and the chamber and barrel would be chrome plated to resist corrosion. Colt would treat steel parts with a phosphate coating to resist rust. The first rifles with these changes would not hit the jungles of Vietnam until late 1967 with the majority being deployed during 1968. By that time, it was too late for Fox Company. Many of the Marines would die on the battlefield due to the M-16 rifle's failure.

By 1970, the old M-16 would be replaced by the new XM16 E1 rifles. It had taken five years for the weapon to become as reliable as originally advertised.

At the end of March and for the next month in 1967, the Second Battalion, Fifth Marines would be issued the new M-16 rifle.

On March 27, 1967, Fox Company of the Second Battalion, Fifth Marines would be the first company in the battalion to receive the new M-16 rifle. That morning, Corporal Barnes was with Fox Company on a reconnaissance patrol. It was in an area outside of the An Hoa combat base.

A helicopter loaded with the new M-16 rifles, magazines and numerous crates of 5.56 mm ammunition landed in a clearing near the Fox Company's position. The troops of Fox Company were ordered to line up at the chopper door and turn in their M-14 rifles with all magazines and ammunition. Corporal Barnes had a feeling of being defeated in battle and was giving up his sword, something that had protected him for the last 12 months. The Marines were handed the new M-16 rifle through the door of the helicopter with magazines and ammunition.

This day would be the faithful beginning of Fox Company's death and pain for many months to come carrying the M-16 rifle.

No one, as so often happens in government, would be held accountable.

You don't use US troops fighting in combat, in the middle of a war, to field test a rifle. Many politicians and military personnel would have blood on their hands for not addressing the problem sooner, but the real blood was left on the battlefields of Vietnam.

FEEDING THE FLAMES

"That which does not kill us makes us stronger."
-Friedrich Nietzsche

5.1 *April Fool's*

April 1, 1967

April Fool's Day: confirmed kill

Fox Company moved to the Phu Loc area of responsibility. The main objective of the outpost was to ensure that Liberty Road all the way to An Hoa remained open. Mines and booby traps were a big problem in the area.

On one occasion, a squad size patrol was headed down Liberty Road when they apprehended three Viet Cong planting mines. During a search of the area, one punji trap with a sign was found. The sign read: *GOOD MORNING, HOW ARE YOU AND HOW DO YOU DO*. It was attached to one of the stakes in the pit. On closer examination, the pit was found to be booby trapped with a M-26 fragmentation grenade. The trap was blown in place.

On April 1, Sergeant Gerald Ackley, the Second Platoon Sergeant came to Barnes, "Hey Rick, I need a machine gun team to volunteer for a patrol. Ten Marines from another platoon are at our perimeter ready to go on a reconnaissance patrol. They failed to bring a gun team with them. They don't want to leave the perimeter without one."

"Ok Sarge, I'll get my team together."

Barnes, by this time, was a gun team leader for a three-man machine-gun team. He didn't know any of the Marines on the patrol except for his gun team. The 10-man team had a lieutenant in charge who he was also not familiar with.

At 1115 hours, the patrol was on its way back to base camp. They were suddenly fired at by a sniper from a tree along the trail. Barnes spotted the sniper in the tree. Taking aim he fired one round from his M-16 rifle. He knew his round made contact when a body fell to the base of the tree.

Barnes headed towards the tree to make sure the enemy soldier was dead. The area was covered with waist high elephant grass which hampered visibility. While moving forward, he moved the elephant grass aside with his left hand keeping his rifle at the ready with his right. Within a short distance, he encountered the wounded Viet Cong. He didn't see the Viet Cong in the elephant grass until he got 10 feet from the soldier.

The round from Barnes' rifle had entered through the stomach area of the soldier, cutting his cartridge belt in half. Looking down, in his left hand the soldier held a chicom grenade. It was wired to a section of the cartridge belt by a piece of com wire. The soldier was in the process of pulling the detonation string from the bottom of the grenade's bamboo handle. Barnes immediately raised his rifle and shot the soldier through his left eye. With additional Marines moving up behind him he hollered, "grenade!" while diving to the ground.

He laid on the ground, waiting for the grenade to explode next to him. After a couple minutes he realized that the grenade apparently had a faulty blasting cap and failed to explode. Viet Cong oftentimes carried their grenades exposed on their cartridge belt to the weather. This would cause the grenade to fall victim to the humid, tropical climate. Moisture would enter through the bamboo handle and into the blasting cap. This made it unable to fire the powder within the grenade. It was a lucky day for Corporal Barnes.

When he got up from the ground, he picked up the soldier's sniper rifle. It was a M-1 Garand, 30 Caliber American made rifle, ser. #5135528. While holding it in his hands, the

Lieutenant on the patrol walked up to Barnes. The Lieutenant looked at Barnes and said, "Give me that rifle."

Barnes replied, "Sir, the kill was mine, it's my rifle."

"Marine, give me the fucking rifle."

Barnes reluctantly gave it to the Lieutenant as he walked away. He thought, *damn, that was a nice rifle and it would have made a nice souvenir*. Looking down at the dead Viet Cong, the chicom grenade was still clenched in the soldier's left hand. *Damn,* he thought, *if I can't have the rifle then I want that grenade*. He walked over and picked up a 6-foot branch lying near a tree. Barnes used the limb to knock the grenade from the soldier's hand.

One of the Marines attached to the patrol was a linguist who could speak and write Vietnamese. While looking for a branch, Barnes saw the Marine writing on a small piece of paper. When finished writing, the linguist rolled the piece of paper in a pencil-like form and struck it in the hole where the sniper's eye once was. Asking the Marine what he wrote on the paper, he stated, "This is what will happen to all you bastards before this war is over."

Barnes knocked the grenade around a couple times on the ground and waited for it to explode, he was relieved when it hadn't. Now came the dilemma of how to get the grenade back to base camp. He realized there would be no choice but to carry it back. Now he had to decide where he could put it so if it did go off it would not kill him in the process. He finally decided to put it in the lower pocket of his fatigue pants. He thought if it did detonate, the worst it would do is take off his leg. He later questioned his rationale with that decision. When he lifted the grenade from the ground and placed it in his pocket without donating, there was a feeling that he had just crossed the finish line of a marathon race.

During the march back to base camp the Marine in front of Barnes and the one behind him kept a long distance away. They knew he could very well be a walking, ticking, time bomb.

Upon returning to base camp, he walked straight to the ordinance section of the battalion. He entered the ordinance tent, "Sergeant, would you remove the blasting cap and powder from this Chicom Grenade?"

The Sergeant looked at Barnes, "Corporal, very carefully put that grenade behind those sandbags over there." It took a few minutes of convincing the Sergeant by retelling the story of how he ended up with the grenade. "Come back in a couple hours and you can pick up the grenade, I'll have it ready."

When Barnes returned to the ordinance tent to pick up the grenade, he carried an old pair of combat boots with him. He placed the grenade in the toe of one of the boots and immediately walked to the post office mail section of the battalion command post. He asked one of the postal clerks if he had some packaging material. He packaged the pair of boots and addressed them to his mother and father back in Indiana. On the outside of the box prior to packaging he placed a note. Mom and Dad do not open this box until I return home. It's just a dirty old pair of boots.

The patrol was another defining moment for Rick. Killing an enemy soldier continued to give him the mental state he needed to survive. During many battles in the jungles of Vietnam, he would be confronted with situations where he had to kill again. It gave him a mindset that told him he must kill or be killed.

5.2 *Purple Heart*

April 1967

Corporal Barnes gets his first Purple Heart

During a Marines 12-month tour of duty he was allowed a five-day R & R (rest and recuperation). There was a list of approved destinations that the Marines could pick from. One of the locations on that list was Hawaii. Most Marines would go to Bangkok, Thailand.

Corporal Barnes, during his first year in Vietnam, had not put in for R & R. During the first week of April, he decided to put in a request. Barnes wanted to meet his wife Susann in Hawaii for five days. The request was immediately approved and he was on a flight headed to Hawaii.

He joked with his gun team when he got back that he never saw Hawaii, only the hotel room.

On the afternoon of April 9, Corporal Barnes entered the perimeter at Phu Loc base camp. He had returned from a perimeter defense patrol. Passing the Fox Company command post, the Company Gunny hollered in the direction of the patrol, "I need someone to ride shotgun on a mail run."

Barnes walked over to the command post area, "Gunny I'll go."

The mail had come in earlier by helicopter to Phu Loc. Once separated, part of the mail had to go down Liberty Road about a mile to an observation post. Every day, two Marines would take the Mail to the observation post on a M274 Mule.

A mule was a quarter ton, flatbed, 4-wheel drive, completely open and exposed. The flatbed offered absolutely no protection to the driver. The Mule was used mainly as a cargo carrier, medium range infantry support vehicle. About 4' x 9' in overall size, it usually had nothing but a seat for the driver; maximum speed was 25 mph.

Corporal Barnes walked into the command post area. Corporal Gary O'Brien, the company's administration clerk, was sitting behind a small folding desk. On top of his desk was a typewriter. In the Marine Corps we jokingly called these Marines, Remington Raiders. They manned the typewriter.

Barnes laid his cartridge belt alongside Gary's desk, "Keep an eye on this for me. I'll pick it up in a little while."

Corporal O'Brien looking up at Barnes said, "Hey, when you get back, would you talk to the Captain for me? I want to get in with machine guns with you guys. I hate what I'm doing. I want to get out where the action is."

"Ok O'Brien, when I get back, I'll see what I can do."

He walked down to the mule where another Marine was putting on his flak jacket. Turning to Barnes he pointed to another flak jacket lying next to the mail bag. "Put that additional flak jacket on the front of your body. I am going to drive full speed down Liberty Road, hopefully going fast enough so if we hit a landmine it will explode behind us. You're the one that's going to need extra protection."

Rick's next thought was, *why do I keep volunteering? Maybe I should be driving...*

The ride to the observation post was uneventful. On the return trip they did receive some incoming sniper rounds, fortunately, they were going fast enough that no rounds made contact.

When Corporal Barnes returned to the command post, he walked over to Gunny Jones. "Hey Gunny, would you speak to the Captain about transferring Corporal O'Brien to guns? I'm short on men and could sure use him."

A week later, Corporal O'Brien was transferred to guns. On their next encounter, Barnes told O'Brien, "The guys call me Barney and we will call you Obie." From that day on, he lost his last name.

CPL Barnes on the steps of a French house at the Nong Son Coal Mines

There was a special relationship between Marines on the battlefield and their Navy Corpsmen. You would hear the call during battle, "Corpsman up!" over the sound of gunfire or the roar of an explosion. The Corpsman would move towards that cry. They would put on a tourniquet, stop the bleeding, clear airways and attempt to prevent shock.

An enemy sniper would shoot a Marine, wait for the Corpsman to show up and have his next target in his sights. The Corpsman was not a Marine, he was part of the Navy Medical Corps, but to Marines, he was a Marine. The Marines took care of them and they took care of the Marines. It was their training, composure and the medical bag that often meant the difference between life or death. They would risk their lives to save another. They fought to hold death at bay.

10,000 Navy Corpsmen served with their Marine brothers in Vietnam. Nearly 1/3 over 3000 would be killed or wounded. In Navy Medical School they were told of their survival odds in serving with the Marines, yet they volunteered. The Corpsman were the Marines' safety net, lifeline in hopes of making it home. Sometimes even their own survival and medical care was up to them.

April 16, at 1115 hours, Corporal Barnes was on a platoon sized patrol outside of Phu Loc. Barnes, while moving down a trail, was 40 feet behind the platoon Corpsman. Looking to his front, he saw the Corpsman walk into a small clearing. Suddenly a large explosion rang out.

Barnes felt what seemed like a nail being driven into his arm, near his elbow.

The Corpsman in front of him had stepped on and detonated a land mine.

Seeing the Corpsman lying prone on his back in the clearing, Barnes ran to his side. Looking down at the Corpsman, the land mine had torn his right leg off right above the knee. Reaching for the medical bag lying next to him, Barnes opened it, trying to find a tourniquet. The Corpsman then raised himself to a seated position, grabbing the bag out of Barnes hands, stating, "I've got it, I've got it."

Barnes watched in disbelief as the Corpsman pulled a tourniquet from his bag and wrapped it around the bleeding stub; what was left of his right leg. He then took a morphine syringe from his bag and stuck it in his leg, above the tourniquet.

Still not believing the poise and composure he had just witnessed while the Corpsman cared for his own leg wound, Corporal Barnes had paid no attention to his arm until the Navy Corpsman was placed into the medevac chopper.

Barnes pulled a sharp shroud of metal about an inch long from his arm near his elbow. The metal had not struck a large blood vessel and little blood was coming from the wound.

When Corporal Barnes returned to Phu Loc with the patrol, he went to see Doc Donovan, the company's Corpsman. Donovan gave him some bacitracin ointment and bandage to help prevent any infection from the wound. When he told Doc Donovan what he had just witnessed earlier, he was still in disbelief.

The mine that was detonated was a M-16A2 type. It explodes instantaneously once you step on and trigger the fuse. The mine was similar to the German S-Mine, also known as the Bouncing Betty, which got its name from World War II troops. It would be buried underground with only the prongs sticking up, making it extremely difficult to spot, particularly in areas of long grass or heavy undergrowth and debris. When detonated, it would rise approximately 2 feet into the air before exploding. Marines dealt with these mines throughout the War.

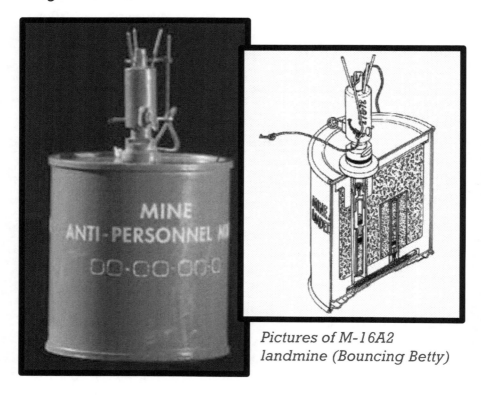

Pictures of M-16A2 landmine (Bouncing Betty)

Six months later, at the Marine Corps Base in Camp Pendleton California, while speaking with the company clerk and checking his records, Barnes found out Company Corpsman Donovan had submitted him for a Purple Heart. In two short months, Doc Donovan would play an important role in Barnes' survival.

5.3 *Enemy Contact Heats Up*

April 18, 1967 (April & May)

Corporal Barnes loses another machine gunner.

During the months of April and May in 1967, everything seemed to be changing for Corporal Barnes. Every ambush, reconnaissance patrol or operation that took place, resulted in numerous casualties within the company. The Que Son Valley was Fox Company's area of operation. The North Vietnamese Army had gained a strong foothold in the valley. They had moved two regiments of the Second NVA Division along with the Third and 31st Regiments into the area. The Marines were now fighting a fully armed and trained Army from North Vietnam. In 1967, almost 1,000 Marines would die in the Que Son Valley. That number was equal to almost 2 battalions of frontline Marines. The NVA lost almost 6,000 soldiers.

Many of the Marines that Barnes fought alongside for months were ready to rotate back to the states. One of his closest friends from Chicago, Sergeant Hank "Ski" Januchowski, was scheduled to rotate in mid-May. Ski was a solid soldier when he came out of Marine boot camp. The two Marines always had each other's back. Sergeant Januchowski seemed to walk the jungles of Vietnam with a protective shield from God almighty himself.

The soldiers that didn't come back from Vietnam were the true heroes. Both Corporal Barnes and Sergeant Januchowski believed strongly in fate; a bullet either had your name on it or it didn't. When the bullets started flying, you had to act accordingly. Sergeant Januchowski was just that Marine. He was respected by both his Commanders and his fellow Marines.

CPL Barnes and SGT Januchowski at An Hoa Base Camp

SGT Hank "Ski" Januchowski

RICK BARNES

Over the past months, Corporal Barnes had lived and fought alongside guys from all over the United States:

-A Hell's Angel, motorcycle rider from California.
-A watermelon farmer from Georgia
-A bull rider from Wyoming
-A hog farmer from Idaho
-A Navajo, Native American, from New Mexico
-A Future Cleveland Browns Linebacker, NFL, football player from Ohio
-A Steel worker from Pennsylvania
-A Mexican American from Abilene Texas
-A Lobsterman from Maine
-An heir to a major mattress company fortune, who defied his father's wishes by joining the Marines to go to Vietnam.

Barnes never fought alongside a Senator or Congressman's son. They would send everyone else's son to fight their war. When they cut a Marine's hair off and put him in a Marine Corps uniform, they all became one family; one brotherhood.

When PFC Mike Hernandez arrived in Vietnam, he quickly found that a lot of the Marines seemed to keep to themselves, no one reached out or tried to get close to one another. They seemed to enjoy time to themselves. However, he noticed there was one thing that brought everyone together—music. Pop music and country music were the most popular. The music of the 1960's would become classics. Mike grew to be friends with guys from Texas during his time in Vietnam. L/Cpl Jesse Manciaz was from Plainview in the panhandle and L/Cpl John Moreno was from Colorado City, west of Abilene. Doc Mauricio Aparicio was from El Paso and PFC King was from Houston. PFC Chris Figueroa, with his Latino accent, was from Puerto Rico. Manciaz was the guy that brought everyone together; his kidding around and smile kept us loose. Manciaz's family would send him the latest

Texan (Tejano) music from home and we would jam to that along with country music during any down time.

On the morning of April 18, 1967, Fox Company, while on a patrol in the Nong Son area, came under heavy small arms fire from a concealed enemy force. One of Corporal Barnes' machine gunners, Lance Corporal John Gobrecht, would be shot in the elbow during the exchange of gunfire. Lance Corporal Gobrecht was medevac'd directly to a hospital ship called The Sanctuary, sitting off the coast of Vietnam.

Lance Corporal Gobrecht had been on the hospital ship for exactly one month when he returned to An Hoa. On May 18, he entered the weapons platoon hut at An Hoa.

Corporal Barnes was the section leader for all machine gun teams in the company. He had recently moved Corporal Perry Jones to the Third Platoon to be the squad leader for the two-gun teams there. Perry Jones greeted John at the entrance to the weapons hut, "Welcome back Hanover, looks like that elbow healed up pretty fast."

John replied, "Yeah, too fast. Did you guys hear about Operation Union I? They brought a shit load of casualties onto the Sanctuary. I got a chance to read a copy of the *Stars & Stripes* and they said the regiment kicked some ass."

PJ replied, "Yeah, I'm just glad Fox Company wasn't on that operation, I heard 110 Marines got their ass killed. John, you know Corporal Barnes here, he gave you the honor of taking over my gun team in Second Platoon."

John, turning to Barnes, said sarcastically with a lopsided grin, "Thanks Barnes, that's just great, exactly what I've been wanting."

"Welcome back John."

On May 18, Fox Company launched a highly successful search and destroy mission. Intelligence had indicated the presence and location of a North Vietnamese Army, Rest and Recuperation (R & R) Center. The company was to head towards the hills in the southeastern area of the TAOR. The objective was located near the Alligator Lake area. They were to spring a raid on the enemy encampment while maintaining an element of surprise. The Second Platoon was selected to be a point on the operation. Several of the Marines within the fire teams were given 81-mm rounds to carry along with their own gear. Corporal Barnes was the Section Leader in charge of all gun teams assigned to the Second Platoon and the entire company. He could go with any gun team in the company that he chose. The Marines in Second Platoon were the guys he grew up with since his arrival in Vietnam. They were the ones he had fought alongside for the past 14 months and the guys he usually tried to stay with. His men had to carry their own M-60 bandoliers and could not carry additional mortar rounds.

Barnes was with Second Platoon and one of his gun teams, they were the point gun that evening. The Marines were using machetes to hack their way through the thick jungle underbrush. Everyone, including the machine gun team, took their rotation at hacking through the jungle with a machete. Eventually Captain Graham wanted to know what the holdup was with the lead platoon. Second Lieutenant Kelsey, who had just arrived in Vietnam, explained how we had to cut our own trail through the jungle ahead. The company started getting heat casualties and medevacs had to be called in. They began to wonder if the element of surprise had been compromised, but the operation continued. The next morning the company turned north and moved along a deep gully that provided cover as they approached the area of Alligator Lake.

By mid-morning, Corporal Barnes and the point gun team stopped. Voices could be heard on the other side of the hedgerow ahead. They moved up to get a closer look. A number of Viet Cong were gathered around a campfire, enjoying a meal and light-hearted conversation. Moving back, the 81-mm mortars were called up and set up on a ridge overlooking the NVA position. 15 to 25 more enemy soldiers with packs, helmets and weapons in light grey uniforms were spotted in the same location as the other soldiers. Second Platoon along with both of Corporal Barnes' machine gun teams moved up into a skirmish line.

The plan of action was to push the enemy soldiers into a barrage of mortar fire. Moving forward, the enemy soldiers began to run. The barrage of 81-mm mortars started firing directly in their path of escape. The Second Platoon held up 25 meters from the barrage, expecting a counterattack. When the fire ended, the Second Platoon counted ten enemy KIA's. No prisoners were taken. A few packs, uniforms, cartridge belts, chicom grenades and documents were found in the area. The Company took up defensive positions for the night on a ridge to the west. Listening posts (LP'S) were sent out for the night, the first being PFC Mike Hernandez and two other Marines. This was not the first time he had been on an LP, but this one was one of the most unsettling.

Many NVA soldiers were still believed to be in the immediate area and a night attack was to be expected. No one slept on the LP. You stared into the darkness waiting to see movement. Your job was to alert the Marines on the line of any movement forward of their position. You did not talk, eat or smoke. If it rained you could not use a poncho. The glare on the wet material of the poncho would give your position away. The LP would take a radio with them. You turned the volume of the radio down. You communicated by pressing the key on the handset. If you are ok, key your handset twice, if the enemy was near, you keyed it three times. If the enemy got to close you sent up a red cluster flare to signal your return to your lines and ran like hell. You not only had to worry about being shot by the enemy on your return but also a nervous Marine on the perimeter. Mike sat looking into the darkness, asking God to let him see daylight.

The next morning, the company turned back towards An Hoa. They had a lot of rice paddies and villages to cover before they hit Liberty Bridge Road. Just prior to reaching the road, they received automatic weapons fire from the tree line to their right. The Marines kept humping, carrying their full gear with packs, weapons and ammunition. The enemy fire was hitting just short of the company's rear column. Corporal Barnes set up a machine gun team on a knoll, returning cover fire. As soon as the Company hit Liberty Road, there were tanks, amtracs and six-by-six trucks, waiting to take the company on to An Hoa.

The effective use of supporting 81-mm mortars coupled with a spirited and tactically sound attack, enabled Fox Company to achieve a major success without suffering one Marine casualty. Just a short two weeks later, Fox Company was not going to be so lucky.

WATCH WHERE YOU STAND

"The object of war is not to die for your country but to make the other bastard die for his."

-George S. Patton

6.1 _Operation Union I_

April & May 1967

Prelude to Fox Company's last stand: Operation Union I

The Marines realized that dominance of the fertile, densely populated Qua Son Basin region astride the Quang Nam-Quang Tin boundary was one of the keys to controlling the five northern provinces of Vietnam. The enemy needed this agriculturally rich and populous area to support operations in the coastal lowlands. Despite numerous operations in the basin by both Marine and ARVN forces, government control could not be obtained.

The principal enemy force in the basin was the Second North Vietnamese Army Division. Although headquarters elements of the division appeared there in July 1966, units of its Third and 21st NVA Regiments did not arrive in force until late February 1967. As the year progressed the Third VC Regiment, also part of the Second NVA Division, joined them after moving north into the region from Quang Ngai Province. The demand for Marine units elsewhere had long denied the permanent assignment of a battalion or larger force to the valley.

Operation Union I was an outgrowth of the 1967 joint combined campaign plan and the requirement for III Marine Amphibious Force to replace the Army Republic of Vietnam units at isolated outposts.

During Operation Union I, April 21 to May 16, the Third Battalion, First Marines, fought the PAVN 21st Regiment near the Marine outpost on Loc Son Mountain for control of the southern part of the Qua Son Valley.

It lasted for 27 days, during which time the Marines killed 865 enemy troops, including a reported 486 who were North

Vietnamese Army regulars of the Second NVA Division. The Marines suffered 110 killed, two missing in action, and 473 wounded.

Although the number of enemy casualties was large, Colonel Houghton believed that the psychological impact of Operation Union I on the population of the basin was even more important. The destruction, the death of hundreds of enemy soldiers, the acquisition of significant quantities of supplies, equipment and weapons, was paramount in the eyes of the people.

Despite this optimistic opinion, enemy influence in the Qua Son Basin was far from erased. Continuing activity substantiated reports that the Third and 31st NVA Regiments were moving back into the basin.

In April 1967, intelligence analysts had noted that three NVA Divisions arrayed along the I Corps Northern border. A fourth was located within 20 miles and another pair was a four to ten day march away. Reconnaissance patrols had reported seeing between 3,000 to 4,000 NVA soldiers in the Que Son Valley.

Operation Union II would be the response.

The above information was taken from the Marines Military Department of Defense book, U.S. Marines and Vietnam, 1967.

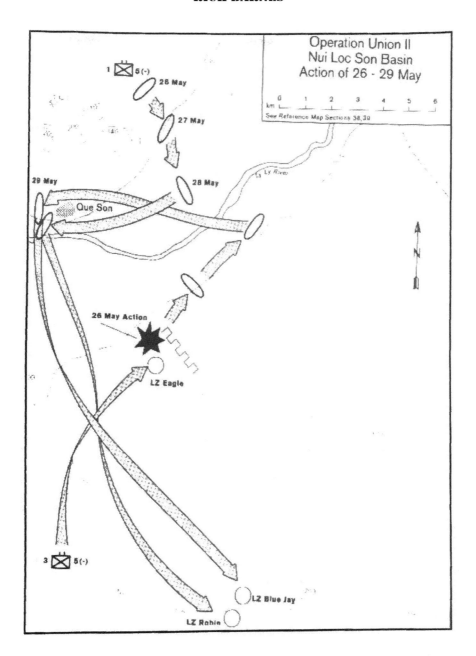

Map from: *US Marines in Vietnam, Fighting the North Vietnamese, 1967*

6.2 *Operation Union II*

May 26, 1967, Operation Union II

We all had fear, we just had a commitment to overcome it.

Operation Union II was designed to be a search and destroy mission in the Que Son Valley. The operation would be carried out by the Fifth Marine Regiment. Launched on May 26, 1967, the operation was to destroy the withdrawing remnants of the Second North Vietnamese Army Division, the Third and 31st Regiments. Intelligence and reconnaissance estimated anywhere between three to 4,000 enemy troops could be expected to still be in the area. These were fully armed and trained North Vietnamese Army units.

The Second NVA Division had been beaten up badly by the Marines in Operation Union I. Major General Hoang Thao was determined to regain superiority in the valley. Thao asked his superior, General Dan Quang Trung, for more troops. Thung was able to intercept an NVA Division headed further south on the Ho Chi Minh Trail. The division was headed further south to fight the U.S. Army. He was given a thousand fresh troops and sent them to the Second Division. These NVA troops would end up being part of the Third Regiment Corporal Barnes and the Fox Marines would fight on June Second.

The plan called for Lieutenant Colonel Hilgartners First Battalion of the Fifth Marines; Lieutenant Colonel Hilgartner only had Alpha and Delta Companies available. He needed a third Company in order to maneuver and deploy a reserve force if needed. Houghton turned to Lieutenant Colonel Jackson, the 2/5 Commander, to nominate his most aggressive company. Fox Company was nominated, with Captain James Graham commanding, to establish blocking positions in the north eastern portion of the valley. The Third

Battalion was to make a helicopter assault into the southern part of the valley and sweep Northeast.

Meanwhile, three battalions of the ARVN (Army Republic of South Vietnam) Ranger Group would attack southwest from Thang Binh, with two units of the Sixth Regiment attacking northwest from a position near Tam Ky. The ARVN named their participation, Operation Lien Ket 106.

The remainder of the Second Battalion, Fifth Marines would be held back guarding our Regimental Base at An Hoa against enemy attack. This kept them out of the Union II Operation. This would prove to be a tactical error.

On the morning of May 26, Lieutenant Colonel Esslinger's Third Battalion, as planned, proceeded with three infantry companies, one weapons company and a command group. They were carried by helicopter to Landing Zone Eagle, an area 5 km east of the Loc Son outpost. The first two waves to arrive at the landing zone experienced only light, small arms fire, but as the bulk of the battalion landed, the LZ was subjected to heavy weapon and mortar fire. An attack by companies Lima and Mike launched to relieve the pressure on the LZ, found a well-entrenched enemy force.

They were identified as being elements of the North Vietnamese Army's Third Regiment. Supported by artillery and airstrikes, Lieutenant Colonel Esslinger's India Company enveloped the enemy's flank, and the Marines soon gained the upper hand. By the late afternoon, the Marines had overrun the last enemy positions. By the end of the day 118 enemy soldiers were killed with the Marines having 38 killed and 82 wounded. The Marines and South Vietnamese Army forces swept the area for the next three days, but contact was minimal as the enemy withdrew from the immediate area. Thinking that the enemy had been routed, the South Vietnamese Army forces ended their part of the operation.

Colonel Kenneth Houghton, a fiery redhead, the commanding officer for the Fifth Marine Regiment, was a highly decorated officer from both World War II and the Korean War. He was not convinced that the North Vietnamese Army had left the Que Son Valley.

FOX COMPANY ENTERS UNION II:

A few days prior To the kickoff of Union II, Captain Graham called Corporal Barnes into the Command hut at An Hoa. "Barnes, I need an acting Platoon Sergeant for weapons platoon, someone to oversee my guns, rockets and mortars on an operation coming up. I've put you in for Sergeant, but you know the bureaucracy, that might take a while. On the upcoming operation you can hang with the command group."

Barnes replied, "Sir, if it's ok with you, can I hang with the Second Platoon."

Graham replied, "Probably not a bad idea Barnes. Lieutenant Kelsey just got here last week, he can probably use you on this upcoming operation. There's a strong possibility of heavy contact with the enemy."

"Thank you, sir, for the confidence."

As Corporal Barnes was leaving the command hut, he passed Lance Corporal Brent "Mac" Mackinnon, who was the Captain's Radioman. It seemed that in Fox Company only the Officers, Platoon Sergeants and the Radiomen knew what was going on at any given time. Everyone else seemed to be in the dark unless you asked one of the three.

Seeing Mac reminded him of a conversation he overheard on a patrol between PFC Sheehy and another Marine. PFC Sheehy had walked over to a Marine who instantly said, "Get the fuck away from me! You're a dead man walking, anyone that gets near you is shot. You're a fucking target."

When a Radioman in training walked into the classroom to learn radio operation, the first thing he saw was a huge number five written on the chalkboard. At least one Marine in the group would get curious and ask, "What does the big five mean?"

The instructor would respond, "That's the life expectancy for your ass, in seconds in a fire fight, so listen up and you might leave here with something that will keep your ass alive when you get to Vietnam." The number was not a scare tactic, it was the grim reality.

Communication was critical to the operations for Union II and throughout Vietnam. Radios were the lifeline for the Marines.

Brent Mackinnon, Fox Company's Radioman, knew that during firefights, it was necessary for platoon and company leadership to communicate. The Radioman had to stay close to leadership. On patrol, the Radioman was shunned and avoided. The antennae not only became a target itself, but identified Officers walking next to the radio. Snipers shot the Officer, the Radioman and then the Machine Gunner in that order. It was inevitable on patrol to her the familiar lament, "Get the fuck away from me!"

Mackinnon knew, "Radiomen were the switchboard for the platoons, battalion, artillery and air communications. They enjoyed a larger perspective of the events surrounding conflict. Many of us are alive today as radios took their hits and shielded us from gunshots and shrapnel. A little-known transcendental benefit was that when you remove the radio and then the flak jacket, you momentarily feel as though you might float straight up and drift away."

Combat platoons had at least two radios, one for the Platoon Commander and one for the Platoon Sergeant. There were also radios for the Company Commander, battalion communications and for the artillery forward observer. The PRC-25, often referred to as "Prick" for short by the grunt, was about the size and weight of a case of beer. With its battery "can" included, it was like a case of beer sitting on top of a six pack and weighed about 24 pounds. In addition to the basic gear of a rifleman, the Radioman carried the radio as well as a spare battery, adding another five or six pounds. Radiomen usually carried smoke grenades to mark locations for gun ships and medevacs.

While most radio operators were fulfilling their MOS, Lance Corporal Mackinnon and PFC Sheehy like many other Marines out of necessity, just had a radio strapped to them because the one before him was shot. This was done often because of the lack of trained operators and their short life expectancy. This would make the radio operator in Vietnam among the most bad-ass troops the Marine Corps had to offer.

On May 27, Fox Company, commanded by Captain James A Graham, was placed under the operational control (OPCON) of the First Battalion, Fifth Marines at 1830 hours.

During the first two days of Operation Union II, May 26-27, Fox was still at An Hoa pulling perimeter duty. Corporal Dennis Sheehy had arrived in Vietnam during the month of March 1967. Shortly after his arrival, during a patrol out of the An Hoa combat base, he would be "volunteered" to carry the radio for Sergeant Ackley of the Second Platoon. Sheehy stated, "Afterwards, he always picked me. I think because I made the mistake of always keeping up with him. After a few times, I just assumed I would be carrying the radio. I even started to like it."

That afternoon, Sergeant Ackley turned to Sheehy, "Dennis, 3/5 got the shit kicked out of them yesterday when they were inserted at LZ Blue Jay. We are going in behind 1/5 in the morning to reinforce them."

Corporal Barnes was in the Second Platoon hut when he got word that Fox was going out on Union early the next morning. Barnes let his gun teams know to carry as many bandoliers of machine gun ammo as possible. He said 3/5 got into a world of shit the day before and we were going in to help them out. Barnes started gathering extra ammo and grenades.

When Barnes was on leave back in February, he had extended his tour in Vietnam. Barnes went into Blythe's gun store in his hometown, Highland, Indiana. He purchased a 1911 A1 45 automatic pistol, same as the one carried by the Marines in Vietnam. After putting it in his luggage and taking it on the plane back to Vietnam, he carried it on patrol during the months of March and April 1967. An order came down from the battalion that personnel were no longer allowed to carry any weapon other than military issued. Barnes had stuck it in his duffel bag. On the morning of the 28th, he went to stick the 45 pistol in his pack. He thought about the battalion order and decided against it. He would later regret that decision as every bullet was about to count.

There was no question that Fox Company was well led. Lance Corporal Brent Mackinnon, who joined Fox 2/5 in the first week of January 1967 as a rifleman in the First Platoon, was transferred to the command post (CP) as Company Radioman in March.

He remembered his first time in the field with the Fox Company Commander, Captain James Graham, "I was his constant companion, shadow, and relay voice to our platoons and weapons people. We came to know each other well. Respected, courageous and popular he continuously studied

127

set reps, maps, and personnel. He was cognizant of the stream of intelligence flowing from various sources. He was, 'born ready' as the saying goes. Captain Graham inspired total confidence. We saw other Company Officers come and go and suffer casualties through horrendous mistakes. He was disciplined both professionally and privately. He carried a Bible and toilet articles in the field when no one else did. He cleansed himself in the mornings. He had a change of fatigues in the middle of nowhere. We were grungy and he would wash, shave, brush his teeth, put on pressed fatigues and there he was, always ready and at his best. We all felt he was the best possible commander in the most difficult times. An aggressive and tactical leader, he enabled Foxtrot to gain a few victories in the midst of chaos and attrition. We had pride in our company and in ourselves," noted Mackinnon.

6.3 *Size Matters*

In Vietnam, on average, a combat platoon would consist of approximately 42 men. In the Fifth Marine Regiment, the platoon was never at full strength.

The following is a breakdown of what each of the platoons in Fox Company would consist of at the beginning of Operation Union II:

The Platoon would consist of three infantry squads. Within that squad you would have three fire teams. Each fire team would consist of three men, that fire team was commanded by a Lance Corporal. Those three fire teams within the squad would be commanded by a Corporal in rank. Each platoon would have a squad of machine guns attached to them. Each of the two gun teams would consist of three men, a gun team leader, a Lance Corporal, machine gunner and assistant gunner/ammo carrier. The two gun teams would have a squad leader, also known as a Corporal. Three additional Marines from the weapons platoon would carry laws rockets.

This platoon would be commanded by either a First or Second Lieutenant. With either a Staff Sergeant or Sergeant as second in command, Platoon Sergeant.

During the battle on June 2, 1967, every Marine in Second Platoon Fox Company would either be killed or wounded. Well over half would be killed.

On May 28, 1967, 154 men of Fox Company would be helo-lifted from the An Hoa airstrip into an LZ in the Que Son Valley. On June 4, 1967, only 64 Marines in Fox Company would return to An Hoa.

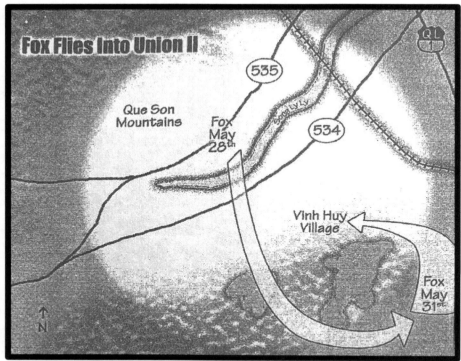

*Photo Courtesy of "Battlelines" by LtCol David Brown

6.4 *On the Tarmac*

May 28, 1967

You don't serve with one Marine, you serve with a company of Marines

0430 HOURS:

The Marine's in Fox Company were up and moving, making final adjustments and additions to their combat gear. Some were seeing that letters they had written to family and loved ones the night before, would get to the company clerk to be mailed home before going out on the operation.

0630 HOURS:

Fox was on the tarmac at An Hoa with all 154 Marines and their attachments waiting for the helo lift to arrive for their transfer to the LZ.

Corporal Barnes was standing with the troopers of Second Platoon when he saw the Platoon Commander, Second Lieutenant Straughan Kelsey, standing next to Lance Corporal James Deasel, his Radioman. The Lieutenant was staring across the tarmac at him. Lieutenant Kelsey had only been in the country for two weeks, straight out of OCS (Officers Candidate School). He definitely looked the part of a boot, straight out of school.

From across the tarmac Lieutenant Kelsey hollered, "Corporal Barnes, I want to talk to you."

Walking over to the Lieutenant, Barnes said, "Sir what can I do for you?" Barnes looked like an old timer, in war years. He had long since stopped worrying about his outward appearance. His jungle utilities had signs of fighting in many red clay fox holes and small tears in various locations. His combat gear was on its last leg. He had the look in his eyes that had long since detached him from the horrors of combat.

"Barnes, I hear you've been here a long time, 15 months I believe. You tell me, how do you stay alive in this shit hole?"

Barnes, looking the boot Lieutenant up and down, "Sir, the first thing you wanna do is take off those brown bars on your collar, we all know you're an Officer. The second thing you wanna do is get rid of that pistol on your hip and get yourself a rifle." Before he could say the third thing, Lieutenant Kelsey was removing his Second Lieutenant bars from his collar. "The last thing you wanna do is keep that Radioman next to you as far away as possible." His Radioman, L/Cpl Deasel, turned with a big smirk on his face, trying not to let the Lieutenant see him laughing.

Barnes began walking back to his earlier position, scanning the tarmac, observing fellow Marines and brothers in full combat gear. Awaiting orders to enter the CH-46 Sea Knights, he hoped that every Marine would stand by him, even until death. He wondered, like every other Marine, is the LZ they were about to go into going to be hot or cold...

0730 HOURS:

Orders were passed to begin entering the CH-46's. The first wave of choppers would take the 1st and 2nd Platoons, along with their weapons platoon attachments. They flew into a landing zone between Highway 535 and the Song Ly to join forces with the rest of the First Battalion. The remainder of the company waited for the second wave.

During our descent into the LZ things started becoming very chaotic. Orders were passed to leave all flak jackets on the helicopter. This became difficult in flight because a lot of combat gear had to be removed in order to remove our flak jackets. Captain Graham was advised at the last minute the rest of 1/5 was not wearing them. He decided Fox was not going to wear theirs either.

PFC Sheehy, Sergeant Ackley's Radioman, was not wearing a shirt or t-shirt under his flak jacket. He immediately realized he was going into battle without a shirt on.

While exiting the helicopter, Barnes hollered to Lance Corporal Gobrecht to set up his machine gun team as part of the LZ security. Corporal O'Brien positioned another machine gun team on the opposite side of the perimeter. The crew aboard the helicopters pushed the Marines out the doors as quickly as possible to get their birds back in the air. Being on the ground made them extremely vulnerable to enemy sniper fire.

The choppers were quickly back in the air and returned to the An Hoa airbase to pick up the second wave and the remainder of Fox Company. On their return, they landed near some waiting trucks across the runway. Large green items were being thrown out the rear doors of the choppers. Initially, many of the waiting Marines thought the items were body bags. With both fear and then anger entering most of their minds, they immediately realized they were going into a hot LZ with casualties. They didn't realize until entering the helicopters it was flak jackets being unloaded. Staff Sergeant Marengo passed the word to his Third Platoon to remove their flak jackets and put them in a pile. He could not believe that it was 1/5's policy to not wear them. Tony knew he was going into battle. While taking his off, he felt naked, like he had just lost a close friend. After the remainder of Fox Company entered the helicopters and lifted off the tarmac, you could see mounds of green flak jackets.

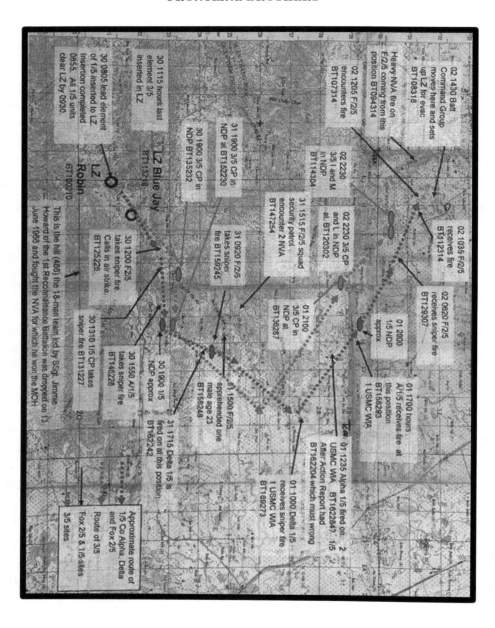

02 1430 Bat Command Group moves here and sets up LZ for evac BT108318

02 1035 F/2/5 receives fire BT112314

Heavy NVA fire on F/2/6 coming from this position BT094314

02 1205 F/2/5 encounters fire BT107314

31 1900 3/5 CP in NDP at BT162230

02 2230 3/5, I and M in NDP BT114304

30 1900 3/5 CP in NDP BT135232

30 1115 lead element 3/5 inserted in LZ

02 2230 3/5 CP and L in NDP at BT120302

31 1515 F/2/5 security patrol encounter 2 NVA BT147254

LZ Blue Jay

30 0805 lead element of 1/5 inserted to LZ Insertion completed 0855. All 1/5 units clear LZ by 0930.

LZ Robin BT160210

31 0920 F/2/5 takes sniper fire BT158245

30 1200 F/2/5 Calls in air strike. BT125228

01 2100 3/5 CP in NDP at BT136287

01 2000 1/5 NDP approx

01 1700 hours A/1/5 receives fire at this position BT156293 1 USMC WIA

This is the hill (488) the 18-man team led by SSgt. Jimmie Howard of the 1st Reconnaissance Battalion was dropped on 13 June 1966 and fought the NVA for which he won the MOH

30 1550 A/1/5 takes sniper fire

30 1310 1/5 CP takes sniper fire BT131227

30 1800 1/5 NDP approx BT146228

31 1500 F/2/5 apprehended one male age 23 BT156248

31 1715 Delta 1/5 is fired on at this position BT162242

01 1235 Alpha 1/5 fired on. 2 USMC WIA. BT162284? 1/5 After Action Report had BT162204 which must wrong

01 1000 Delta 1/5 receives sniper fire 1 USMC WIA BT18273

Approximate route of 1/5 Co Alpha, Delta and Fox 2/5 Route of 3/5 Fox 2/5 & 1/5 sites 3/5 sites

RICE PADDIES & VALLEYS

"Even though I walk through the valley of the shadow of death, I will fear no evil, for you are with me."

-Psalm 25:4

7.1 *Prelude to Battle*

May 28, 1967

It was not victory or satisfying the chain of command that the Marines fought so hard, but their devotion to one another.

0830 HOURS:

The LZ was secured and Fox Company began moving a short distance onto a grassy knoll. 15 - 20 North Vietnamese troops in camouflage uniforms were observed moving southwest approximately 1100 meters away. An artillery mission of 105 mm HE was fired on the enemy target. The area was searched and a tunnel complex was found. The tunnels were approximately four feet in diameter and ten feet deep. The Marines searched the tunnels with negative results. Fox Company set into a defensive perimeter for the night.

May 29, 1967
1220 HOURS:

The Company again made contact with 7 NVA wearing packs and helmets running through a tree line approximately 400 m away. Artillery was called in. The area was searched with negative results.

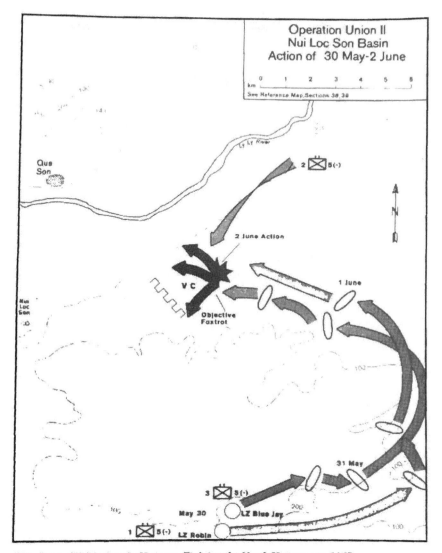

Map from: *US Marines in Vietnam, Fighting the North Vietnamese, 1967*

May 30, 1967

With only light contact being made by the battalion, Colonel Houghton, the Regimental Commander, implemented a new action plan. He did not believe all the NVA forces had left the Que Son Valley. The First Battalion's Alpha and Delta Companies along with Foxtrot Company, were to be helo lifted into LZ Robin. The order was to change the direction of the attack towards the hills along the southern rim of the valley.

At first light that morning, Fox Company boarded UH 34s and began a helicopter assault across the treetops of the valley. The early morning dew was rising from the jungle floor. With the Marines of Fox in full battle gear, the only thing missing was the Creedence Clearwater revival song, *Fortunate Son*.

The battalion's mission was to maneuver around the mountains to the north and then west towards the village of Vinh Huy. The end objective would be codenamed Objective Foxtrot. The village was just three km east of where 3/5 had fought their major battle on May 26. On May 30, the battalion was to secure Objective A.

1130 HOURS:

Fox Company moved down the mountain side and into the valley towards Objective A. Sniper fire was received from approximately six to ten enemy soldiers 400 meters to the north. Fox Company returned fire and called in airstrikes. Coming in low through the valley was an A4E Crusader to drop its payload. The pilot clipped a tree and flipped into the mountain valley wall. Watching the jet aircraft erupt into a ball of flames was a disheartening sight for Corporal Barnes and the Marines around him. The pilot did not have time to eject.

When Fox first landed in LZ Robin, an artillery forward observer (FO) with his Radioman, was assigned to the company. The Captain put him in S/Sgt Tony Marengo's Third Platoon. During the first couple days, it was becoming apparent that both the FO and his Radioman were having difficulty keeping up in the heat. Marengo tried to assist them both in carrying their gear. It was starting to cause Tony's Platoon to lag too far behind and hold up the forward movement of the company. The company was having trouble keeping up with the battalion's objective. The need finally came to medevac the FO and his Radioman due to heat exhaustion. It would be a great loss in the days to come. An Officer and his Radioman to call in air and artillery support for Fox Company was about to become a matter of life or death.

1910 HOURS:

The battalion secured objective A and a night perimeter was established.

May 31, 1967
0920 HOURS:

That morning, small arms fire was received from a number of enemy soldiers approximately 300 m to the north. Lance Corporal John Gobrecht, with his gun team, was to the left of Barnes. PFC Robert Mills, his machine gunner, began laying down suppressive fire when an enemy round threw dirt in his eyes. Gobrecht raised and attempted to assist PFC Mills in clearing his eyes.

Gobrecht suddenly hollered, "Barnes I'm hit! Blood is running down my back!"

Crawling over to John's side, Corporal Barnes could see where the round had entered his pack. His fatigue shirt was wet, but it did not appear to be blood. Upon opening

139

Gobrecht's pack, Barnes found that the round had entered a can of c-rations and the liquid from the can leaked through his pack and onto his back.

Relieved Gobrecht stated, "Wow, Barnes, that was a close one."

A short time later, Fox Company again received sniper fire, one enemy soldier was killed and heavy blood trails were found. The company set into a night perimeter for the evening.

June 1, 1967
0800 HOURS:

Second Platoon was awaiting orders from the battalion to move out. Lieutenant Kelsey had finished shaving using his helmet as a sink with a small amount of water. Turning to PFC Sheehy, his Platoon Sergeants Radioman, "Sheehy, would you like to use my razor and helmet to shave?"

"Sure Lieutenant."

After shaving, PFC Sheehy saw Lieutenant Kelsey reading what appeared to be a book of plays, Shakespeare perhaps.

Lt Kelsey turned and asked, "Would you like to read my book?" Sheehy accepted his offer, reading for about a half hour until the company moved out. Sheehy was surprised at the Lieutenants actions. The morning before he had gotten his ass chewed out for taking too long making a cup of coffee. Orders had been given to move out and Sheehy didn't have his shit together. After interacting with Lieutenant Kelsey, PFC Sheehy felt that maybe Second Platoon was in good hands with Kelsey in charge.

Lieutenant Colonel Hilgartner moved Fox Company abreast and to the left of Delta Company. Alpha was moved to the rear of Fox. They were to be the reserve company with the First Battalion's Command Group.

By the afternoon, both battalions reached the edge of the Que Son Valley. They moved northwest towards the site of the original May 26 battle.

Nearing the end of Fox Company's objective, Corporal Barnes was starting to think that maybe the Third and 21st Regiments of the North Vietnamese Army had eluded the Marines. He would soon learn that wasn't the case...

In High School history class, Rick Barnes, had been given an assignment to memorize the poem, The Charge of the Light Brigade. Soon Fox Company and the 1st Battalion would be reliving those words in the poem written on, December 2nd , 1854.

7.2 *Into the Valley of Death*

POETRY FOUNDATION

The Charge of the Light Brigade

BY ALFRED, LORD TENNYSON

I

Half a league, half a league,
Half a league onward,
All in the valley of Death
  Rode the six hundred.
"Forward, the Light Brigade!
Charge for the guns!" he said.
Into the valley of Death
  Rode the six hundred.

II

"Forward, the Light Brigade!"
Was there a man dismayed?
Not though the soldier knew
  Someone had blundered.
  Theirs not to make reply,
  Theirs not to reason why,
  Theirs but to do and die.
  Into the valley of Death
  Rode the six hundred.

III

Cannon to right of them,
Cannon to left of them,
Cannon in front of them
  Volleyed and thundered;
Stormed at with shot and shell,
Boldly they rode and well,
Into the jaws of Death,
Into the mouth of hell

Rode the six hundred.

IV

Flashed all their sabres bare,
Flashed as they turned in air
Sabring the gunners there,
Charging an army, while
  All the world wondered.
Plunged in the battery-smoke
Right through the line they broke;
Cossack and Russian
Reeled from the sabre stroke
  Shattered and sundered.
Then they rode back, but not
  Not the six hundred.

V

Cannon to right of them,
Cannon to left of them,
Cannon behind them
  Volleyed and thundered;
Stormed at with shot and shell,
While horse and hero fell.
They that had fought so well
Came through the jaws of Death,
Back from the mouth of hell,
All that was left of them,
  Left of six hundred.

VI

When can their glory fade?
O the wild charge they made!
  All the world wondered.
Honour the charge they made!
Honour the Light Brigade,
  Noble six hundred!

142

June 2, 1967
0430 HOURS:

It was my duty to kill the enemy, I don't regret it...

Corporal Barnes and Fox Company awoke and prepared to saddle up and move out at first light. Both battalions, 1/5 and 3/5, were within reach of their destination. They began their move northwest towards their objective near the site of the original Union II Battle at LZ Eagle. Once inserted, they circled in a counterclockwise fashion to the complex of mountains positioned to the north of the LZ. Many of the hills were over 400 m high, the highest at 479 m. Streams of cold water were coming down from the deforested slopes. The Marines traversed the thick jungle, interspersed with narrow valleys of tall grass and paddies.

In three days of difficult marches across rough terrain, the Marines covered 16 km since being inserted into LZ Robin. They were weighted down with gear, extra ammo, water and under constant threat of enemy attack. The objective was now only 4 km away, across relatively flat terrain. It was not going to be an easy stroll across the paddy that day.

In the last three days the Marines of both battalions had been shot at and engaged by small groups of the NVA. They had called in artillery and airstrikes with numerous enemy KIA's. Six Marines were wounded, 3 from Alpha 1/5, 1 from Delta 1/5 and 2 from 3/5, they had suffered no KIA's as of yet. After five days on the operation, Fox Company was unscathed. They had suffered cuts from brush, sprains from the rocky ground and had been bitten by leeches and bugs but nobody had been wounded by enemy fire. That was soon to change.

Corporal Barnes and Lance Corporal John Gobrecht's machine gun team, with Second Platoon, took point. First and then Third Platoon brought up the rear of the formation. Fox was only three to four hours to its objective, which was 4000 m to the northwest. Their mission was to secure the three Vinh Huy Villages. Fox Company's final objective, codenamed Objective Foxtrot, was the hamlet at Vinh Huy 2. It was part of an old destroyed French Village split by the same unmarked dirt road that stretched two km between the objectives. Delta Company's objective was Chau Lam 5, to the north of Vinh Huy 2 and to the right flank of Fox Company. Alpha Company would move in a westerly direction towards the hamlet Chau Lam 5 as a reserve company.

The terrain in the objective area of Thang Binh Valley was composed of rice paddies surrounded by dense forests and mountains with elevations of 100 to 479 meters. The rice paddies were interspersed with hills thickly covered with brush.

What the Marines of Fox Company didn't know was they were about to take on a Regimental size enemy force of over 2,000 highly trained and well-disciplined North Vietnamese Army troops. They were willing to defend the headquarters of the Third NVA Regiment centered in the Vinh Huy 2 Village to the last man.

The main battlefield of Vinh Huy 2 was about to become infamous to the Marines of Fox Company as the main killing ground.

Every Marine of Fox 2/5 would soon be in their own desperate fight for survival, as the battle ahead turned out to be one of the deadliest battles of the Vietnam War.

0620 HOURS:

Corporal Barnes, with the lead machine gun team, began receiving small arms fire from an undetermined number of enemy soldiers 550 m to the Northeast. At the time this was thought to be an attempt by the NVA to delay Fox Company's advancement.

As Lieutenant Colonel Hilgartner's First Battalion was nearing its objectives at Vinh Huy 1, Delta Company had to pass through Fox Company. As they passed one another on the trail, Lance Cpl Wayne Puterbaugh from Delta looked over and saw Cpl Victor Driscoll whom he had gone through boot camp with. The two Marines talked for a few minutes as the companies passed. Driscoll was killed later that afternoon fighting in the tree line of Objective Foxtrot.

The three companies moved into a typical attack formation with two companies up and one back.

Delta Company was approximately 1,000 m to the right of Fox Company, but out of visual sight. Alpha Company was to the rear of Fox with the battalion's command group, also out of sight, as reserve.

0800 HOURS:

Delta Company observed two uniformed NVA crossing the open rice paddy to its front. The two soldiers were coming from the direction where Fox Company was located. Both were taken under fire and found dead in the rice paddy later as Delta advanced. Delta Company called for airstrikes to its immediate front of their position.

0930 HOURS:

Two lead companies of the Third Battalion's, Fifth Marine Regiment, commanded by Lieutenant Colonel Charles B. Webster, were under heavy fire from 200 well dug-in North Vietnamese troops. They were located over 1,000 m east of Fox Company's location.

After savage fighting and extensive use of supporting arms, the Marines overran the positions. As the companies of the Third Battalion consolidated and began to evacuate their casualties, an evac helicopter took a direct hit from a 57 mm recoilless rifle, killing one Marine and wounding seven others.

01030 HOURS:

Corporal Barnes with the lead machine gun team, was entering the area of Objective Foxtrot, between Hills A and B.

Terry Klein, a rifleman in the Third Platoon, was the last man in the column and bringing up the rear. He passed by a cave to his left that contained two wooden benches. Staff Sergeant Tony Marengo, Third Platoon Sergeant, with a usual cigar in his mouth and carrying a shotgun, walked back to Klein. Pointing the barrel of the shotgun towards the cave, "Terry, throw two grenades in the cave and let's get moving."

Corporal Barnes along with Corporal Tom McDonald's lead squad of Marines in the Second Platoon, moved into a small clearing between Hills A and B. Word was passed through Second Platoon that a bird dog plane—a small U.S Army, single prop, fixed wing plane—flying overhead had spotted enemy movement up ahead.

The distinctive "Ack, Ack" sound of the AK-47 opened up. There was no mistaking the unique signature of the devastating automatic weapon. The North Vietnamese Army carried the AK-47. Corporal Barnes and the Marines of Second Platoon heard the unmistakable automatic clatter. Looking up towards Hill B, Barnes saw an American Marine's helmet roll down along a group of boulders. Lance Corporal Dan Yeutter, along with some of the Marines from Corporal Tom McDonald's squad, had moved up the side of the rock formation and started climbing over and around the large boulders littering the face of the hill. Running up the side of the rock formation, Corporal Barnes found Yeutter laying on a rock outcropping with two bullet holes across his chest. A bullet had hit the machine gun bandolier around his chest, deflecting at an angle into his chest, coming out his side and reentering his arm. The wounds were in the lung area and with every attempt to breathe, Yeutter was gasping for air.

Three or four Marines had followed Barnes up the hillside. "Who's got cigarettes?" Barnes called out, over the clatter of more AK-47's in the distance. Instantly, several c-ration cigarette packs flew towards the boulders and the wounded Marine. With the scent of gun smoke in the air, Corporal Barnes tore the cellophane off the cigarette packs, placing cellophane over each blood-soaked hole on Yeutter's chest.

The Marine once again, began to breathe as the Corpsman Doc Schmit landed alongside Barnes, "Barnes, I got this."

Barnes rose and continued up the side of the boulders. Nearing the top of the biggest boulder, he could see Lance Corporal McAnaly standing in some overhanging brush to his right.

"Barnes," McAnaly warned and pointed, "there's one right around the corner of the rock you're leaning against."

Before either Marine could react, a chicom grenade with a bamboo handle came flying around the boulder and landed in front of McAnally. With a deafening blast, Barnes felt a tear across his forearm and heard McAnaly call out, "Barnes I'm hit!"

With his ears still ringing from the grenade's concussion, Barnes pulled an American grenade from his web gear and tossed it around the boulder. A blast and a glance around the boulder revealed a fallen North Vietnamese soldier, unmistakably dead.

Three North Vietnamese soldiers were making their way down the boulders and headed towards the open rice paddy. Barnes called for Lance Corporal Gobrecht's gun team to put suppressive fire on the fleeing soldiers. Looking back at the dead Vietnamese soldier, Barnes could see a shallow cave with blankets and military gear scattered around.

He ran to the edge of Hill B where Gobrecht had his gun team set up, 10 to 15 NVA soldiers were being cut down by Lance Corporal Gobrecht's gun team and members of Varena's squad as they attempted to enter the rice paddy.

L/CPL Dan Yeutter

L/CPL Carl McNally

Second Platoon Commander, Second Lieutenant Kelsey hollered, "Sheehy, get a couple of guys and move these two wounded into that open area" pointing to a section. Then turning to his Radioman, Lance Corporal Deasel, Kelsey ordered, "Call in a medevac chopper right away."

As soon as the chopper landed, Lance Corporal McAnaly and Second Lieutenant Knight, the Third Platoon Commander, got onto the chopper.

Lance Corporal Yeutter was placed on the floor of the chopper. The Marine was still alive, but his ashen face and labored breathing made his chance of survival seem slim. As the helicopter lifted off and disappeared, the wounded Marine became a fading memory for most Marines in the platoon. They would not know if he lived or died. They just figured they would never see him again. In any case, his fate was now a reality while there's was still unknown.

149

While the medevac chopper was being loaded, another chopper landed briefly and dropped off a "Kit Carson Scout" to join Fox for the day. Truong Kinh was prematurely wrinkled at the age of 35. Kinh had defected from the Viet Cong last July. After training by the Marine Corps, he had been designated a Kit Carson Scout, in Vietnamese, Hoi Chanh Vien—a term loosely translated as members who have returned to the righteous side.

"Skipper?" First Sergeant Lee asked, "What the hell are we gonna do with him?"

Graham stated, "I'm going to pass him on to Marengo and Third Platoon so keep an eye on him till I get a hold of Tony."

7.3 *The BloodBath Begins*

"Come on you sons of bitches, do you want to live forever!?"
-Sgt. Maj. Daniel Daly (USMC)

The normal reaction under fire was fear. That fear became one of our biggest allies. It kept us thinking and moving forward.

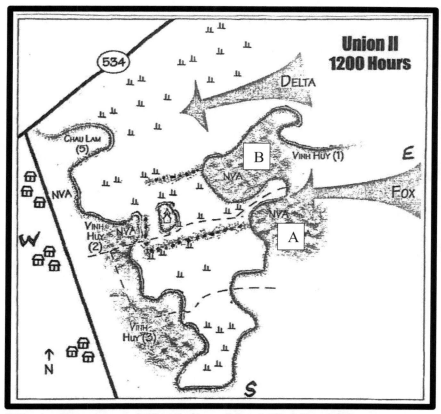

Photo Courtesy of "Battlelines" by LtCol David Brown

When Lance Corporal Gobrecht's gun team and Corporal Ted Varena's Squad opened up on the NVA fleeing down the face of Hill A, Corporal Tom McDonald's squad had also moved to the edge of the hill.

As the enemy soldiers entered the rice paddy, Corporal Tom McDonald, L/Corporal Art Byrd, PFC McCandless, PFC Mike Hernandez, PFC Legere, PFC Wainscott and L/Corporal Searfoss, along with L/Corporal Westphal's fire team, opened up on the soldiers as they decided to run rather than fight. The bodies of the wounded and dead NVA were scattered from the edge of the tree line nearly 40 m into the paddy.

The enemy soldiers were clad in full khaki uniforms. Their packs were filled with rocket propelled grenades, RPGs, AK-47 munitions and 82 mm mortar rounds. They were young with clean uniforms and high and tight haircuts. When PFC Mike Hernandez reached the base of the hill, he could see a Marine standing near an NVA soldier with his hands up. The Marine hollered, "My rifle is jammed!"

Another Marine ran up. Thinking he was in trouble and he shot the enemy soldier point blank.

Second Lieutenant Kelsey motioned to Sheehy, "Tell Fox Six that the first squad just bagged 15 NVA in the paddy in front of Hill B."

Lance Corporal Dennis Sheehy, the Second Platoon radio operator turned to Sergeant Gerry Ackley, "So tell me Sarge, how does it feel to be out in the bush on your last day of your six month extension. Weren't you supposed to fly home today?"

"Pay attention to where you're going, Sheehy, and tell Lieutenant Kelsey that the Company CP has caught up with us. I'm going back and giving this piece of comm wire we found to the Skipper, let's see what he makes of it."

Captain Graham only needed one look at the communications wire to realize it was used by the NVA in their defensive positions. The enemy was waiting for them. Knowing his lead platoon was about to enter the same rice paddy in which Delta was already engaged with the enemy, he ordered his radio operator, Lance Corporal Mackinnon, to have the company hold up.

From the vantage point through the trees, Graham could see to the far side of the rice paddy. What he didn't know was that on the other side of the paddy, two well dug-in and concealed machine guns manned by soldiers of Major Dao Cong's Second Battalion, 31st NVA Regiment were waiting to gun down the Marines in the First and Second Platoons. He decided to call for air and artillery support before moving across the paddy.

"Sir," Corporal Cox, the forward observer stated, "battalion said that air and artillery support would not be available. They've already prepped the area."

Graham said defiantly, "That's bull, you call Tam Ky directly for air prep fire," Then, turning to his battalion radio operator, "Corporal Dirickson, let me speak to Millbrook 6," referring to Lt Col Hilgartner.

"Sir, I have Colonel Hilgartner on the radio," Dirickson offered.

"Millbrook 6, this is Fox 6, over."

"Roger Sir, I can't send my company across that rice paddy unless I prep the area first. I need air or artillery support, the prep fire was a long time ago, over."

"I spoke to Delta 6 before he came under fire and he said he didn't get this far south."

"Yes, I know Delta is getting beat up over there, but unless we get some support right now, we'll get beat up as well, over."

"Well at least let me have one round of artillery to register." For the Artillery Battery to hit the objective accurately, the one Howitzer round would, when called to do so, allow the Battery to hit the objective immediately with rounds, using the same registration data.

"Aye, Aye, Sir."

Gysgt Green and LCpl Mackinnon could hear the disgust in Graham's voice. Captain Graham stared at nothing, managing his frustration. To no one he blurted in disbelief. "He just gave me a direct order to move out."

Direct orders were only given to subordinates when they did not understand or were tending to refuse the direction of the senior. There was no question in the minds of the three of them that complying with the direct order without prep fire was tantamount to suicide.

Captain Graham advised First Platoon to follow the path between Hills A and B, then to bear right as soon as they hit the rice paddy and if possible, to tie in with Delta Company. Second Platoon was advised to move down the face of Hill B, cross behind First Platoon and come on line to their left for the final assault. Third Platoon will be held to the rear as reserve.

"All right, let's move out," Graham advised over the radio.

Sergeant Ackley told the Marines around him, "Follow Lieutenant Kelsey." As Ackley's Radioman, Sheehy, reached the tree line bordering the paddy, he noticed the First Platoon had already entered the rice paddy and was moving towards the right flank. He proceeded to enter the paddy, crossing a trench line running perpendicular.

Looking over, he noticed a Marine. It was the same Marine that had passed out after giving blood on Okinawa during a stopover on their way to Vietnam. Sheehy remembered the Marine rolling down the steps after leaving second floor infirmary. He had cut his head and face in several places, missing the flight to Vietnam the next day. Now, here he was, his head still covered with fresh-looking scars. There was no time for either one to inquire about the other as they stepped out into the paddy.

1300 HOURS:

As Captain Graham neared the area of First and Second Platoons, he directed First Sergeant Lee to move the wounded prisoners to the rear of the column with Third Platoon, "Get the POWs ready to be choppered out to the rear. Stay with Staff Sergeant Marengo. If you need me, call me on the radio."

"Good luck Sir"

Corporal Rick Barnes with Lance Corporal Gobrecht's gun team began to maneuver towards the left flank. The First Platoon was tying in with the Second Platoon.

1310 HOURS:

Kinh, the Kit Carson Scout, had wandered up near the First Platoon's location. He pointed his rifle 30 to 40 meters ahead of him scanning the area.

Gobrecht observed the Scout and motioned to his Section Leader Corporal Rick Barnes, "Hey, Rick," he whispered, "look at that Scout over there behind the First Platoon."

Barnes had no sooner turned, when he witnessed Kinh fire six rounds without hesitation into the field. The straw flew into the air as the rounds impacted the ground. The Scout moved towards the impact area, firing three more rounds.

Gobrecht moved towards the Scout as he witnessed another area that looked similar to the area that Kinh fired into. Looking intently, he opened up with a short burst from his M-16 Rifle. Barnes moved up and with his M-16 nudged the grass that covered the spider trap, finding two dead enemy soldiers.

It was evident they were waiting to open up on the backs of both Platoons. They were part of the back door of the ambush. Once the company had moved into the rice paddy, they were going to close the door by shooting Marines from the rear. This would force the NVA to execute the ambush a bit early on the Second Platoon.

As Corporal Barnes moved further to the left flank of the assault line, he moved to the left of Lieutenant Kelsey. Lance Corporal Gobrecht's gun team was to the left of Barnes, Corporal Gary O'Brien the Second Platoon squad leader for guns was to the left of Gobrecht's team and Lance Corporal Jerry Westphal's fire team. To his left was the rest of Corporal McDonalds squad. These Marines made up the far-left flank of the assault line.

While moving into position, Barnes walked up to a wounded NVA soldier laying in the rice paddy. It was evident the soldier was dying. Corporal Barnes put the barrel of his rifle against the soldier's head ready to pull the trigger.

Lieutenant Kelsey turned Just as Barnes was ready to squeeze, "Barnes! Don't you pull that trigger. Let him be." As the lieutenant turned away, Barnes again put his barrel against the enemy's head, "Barnes! I ordered you not to shoot him."

Not wanting to turn his back on an enemy soldier that was still alive, Barnes leaned down, searching the soldier for any hidden weapons, grenades or military documents. Pulling out a small leather folder, he opened it. A picture fell out onto the soldier's chest. It was a wedding picture of the dying soldier in uniform, standing alongside his wife. Looking at the soldier's left hand, Barnes saw a wedding band. Reaching down, he removed the ring, placing it on his small finger alongside his own wedding band. Barnes knew the young soldier was near death. He would never be able to understand why he removed that ring. It certainly was not for monetary gain. They were simply two, young, married soldiers on opposite side of a war; same battlefield, different worlds.

The ring stayed on Barnes' finger for the next five years before he could remove it from his hand. He still possesses the ring to this day.

7.4 *Into the Jaws of Death, Into the Mouth of Hell*

God gave his worst battle to his strongest Marines

1330 HOURS:

First and Second Platoons had maneuvered online for their final assault. First was in the rice paddy directly in front of Hill B and Second was positioned to the front of Hill A, to their left flank.

Lance corporal Ken "Big Eyes" Reynolds was the pointman for Corporal Conley's Squad in Third Platoon.

Entering the rice paddy behind Second Platoon as the reserve, they began to skirt closely along Hill A. Reynolds stopped dead in his tracks and turned back to Conley. He held his M-16 over his head with the barrel pointed towards the top of Hill A, whispering, "Hey Chuck, we have company, I saw movement up there."

Conley motioned for his fire team leaders to get the squad back through the bamboo tree line bordering Hill A. Conley contacted Third Platoon Commander, Staff Sergeant Marengo on his squad radio. "Fox Three, this is Three Alpha, we saw movement on the top of Hill A. I'll go check it out."

Instantly, Marengo relayed the message to the Company Commander, Captain Graham. "Fox 6, we spotted movement on the top of Hill A, request permission to go check it out."

"That's a negative Fox 3, the hill is already secured, I don't want you to get too far behind, we have already begun our assault."

"Roger 6, I'll pull them back out," Marengo replied.

Second Lieutenant William Knight was Third Platoon's
Commander going into Union II. It was sometime during this
time frame that Lt. Knight advised Staff Sergeant Marengo
that he had to return to the command post area. Marengo
assumed command of the Third Platoon. Tony would later
find out that the Lieutenant had been wounded and
medevac'd out on one of the first medevac choppers.

1350 HOURS:

Unknown to Fox Company, they had just positioned
themselves in the middle of a rice paddy and a horseshoe
ambush. They were surrounded by enemy troops of the
Third NVA Regiment.

2,000 highly trained, well-disciplined and heavily equipped
enemy soldiers, ready to defend Vinh Huy to the last man,
was directly to the front of First and Second Platoon's
location. The Second Platoon, being on the far left flank, was
at the center of the U in the horseshoe; the most vulnerable
spot. There would be no way out for Second Platoon Foxtrot,
it was about to become one of the deadliest battles in the
Vietnam War. The Second Platoon was about to lose more
Marines in the next four hours from one platoon than any
other battle in Vietnam.

The enemy had dug trench lines and spider traps bordering
the half circle of the rice paddy. Numerous tunnel systems
interlaced throughout their defensive positions. This would
enable the enemy soldiers to move freely throughout the
positions and have concealment from Air Power.

The Third NVA Regiment had developed a base camp with
full intentions of standing to fight any Marine unit that dared
to enter the jaws of the tiger.

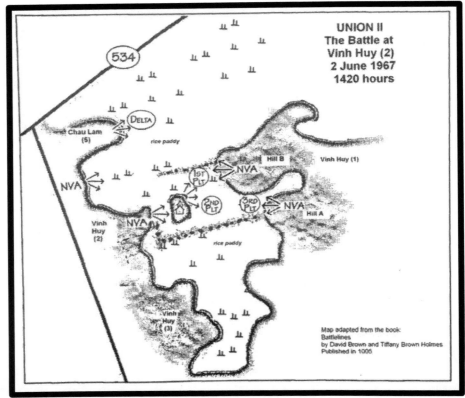

Photo Courtesy of "Battlelines" by LtCol David Brown

1420 HOURS:

In the heat of the afternoon sun, Second Platoon had reached 200 m to the front of the hedge row bordering the Vinh Huy 2 Village. Due to the angle of the rice paddy, First Platoon was still about 250 m away.

Corporal Rick Barnes was moving forward with Second Platoon. He was positioned on the far-left flank with Lieutenant Kelsey directly to his right, Corporal Gobrecht's gun team to his immediate left. Further to the left of the gun team was machine gun Squad leader Corporal Gary O'Brien.

To O'Brien's left was Lance Corporal Jerry Westphal's fire team and the remainder of Corporal McDonalds squad.

Corporal Barnes wiped his face and the sweat from his eyes with his hand as the hot afternoon sun beat down on the steaming rice paddy.

Suddenly, from the hedge row to the front, came the crack of AK-47's whistling past their heads like they had just walked into a beehive full of pissed off bees. The bullets were kicking up dirt and dust everywhere. Two .51 Caliber machine guns, normally used against anti-aircraft or long range sniper rifles, opened up to the front of both First and Second Platoons. Another NVA machine gun, located on Hill A, opened up with devastating fire into the backs of the Second Platoon. The bullets flew by, sounding like someone had just snapped a bullwhip.

A .51 caliber round struck the chest of Lance Corporal Deasel, blowing through the platoon radio strapped on his back. Lieutenant Kelsey's Radioman was dead and his radio useless.

Corporal Ted Varena, a Squad leader in Second Platoon, was lying against a low paddy dike as his platoon was systematically being cut to pieces. Live rounds popped in his ears as they flew by his head and helmet. Bullets tore into his helmet and shirt. To his left, an American M-26 grenade exploded. A machine gun round had impacted the grenade on a Marine's web gear. Barnes saw the flash of the grenade and the plume of white smoke rise as he heard the Marine screaming and thrashing in the paddy. The ground turned red around Corporal Varena. He lost control, stood up and grabbed an M-60 Machine gun from PFC Johnson, who had just been shot through both legs. Varena fired two bursts in the general direction of the enemy gun position before a bullet hit him in the head and knocked him off his feet, blood running into his eyes. Blinded by the wound he tossed back-

and-forth in the loose dirt as he succumbed to the searing pain. Numbness set in over his entire body and the sounds of the battle faded from his consciousness.

Barnes fired his M-16 towards the trench line to his front. The "Whoosh" sound of a B40 RPG (rocket propelled grenade) round landed 25 feet to his front with a loud explosion. He felt a sharp pain to his right calf and searing pain to his right hand, revealing one of his knuckles had been sheared off. Looking down the line of assaulting Marines, he could see rounds ripping into their bodies. It was mass confusion trapped under a blanket of bullets.

The Marines took cover behind the low, two foot high, paddy dikes.

The dead and wounded Marines littered the rice paddy. The First Platoon Commander, Second Lieutenant Schulz, lay mortally wounded. His radio operator, Corporal Lloyd Woods, realized that his Lieutenant was exposed to the intense enemy machine gun fire. Jumping up he made a charge through a hail of machine gun fire reaching his Lieutenant. Hoisting him onto his shoulders he carried him to a safe position behind a paddy dike. Rallying four Marines, along with Corporal James Hester, they sprinted across the open rice paddy attempting to evacuate another wounded marine near an enemy machine gun. Reaching the wounded man, Woods realized moving him would be impossible because of the gunfire. Ignoring the rounds hitting all around him he crashed into the tree line towards the enemy. Woods fired his M-16 until it was out of bullets, killing the stunned soldier. He picked up the enemy's machine gun, killing the second gunner. Using the machine gun, he provided cover for Corporal Hester and the other Marines to evacuate the wounded men.

Corporal Lloyd Woods would receive the Navy Cross for his actions on the battlefield that day and Corporal James Hester would receive the Silver Star for his actions.

PFC Moser, a Radioman with First Platoon, realizing that the lead squad to the front of the Platoon had no communications with the platoon leader, ran 100 yards across the exposed paddy under heavy enemy fire to bring the lead squad communications. After arriving at the squad's position, he saw a wounded Marine lying in the rice paddy. Subjected to intense enemy fire, he ran to the wounded Marine to offer first aid. As he was carrying the wounded Marine back to the squad position, he was killed. PFC Moser was 20 years old when he died.

PFC Keith Moser received the Silver Star posthumously for his actions on the battlefield that day.

Word was passed to Sergeant Ackley from Lieutenant Kelsey to have any Marines move towards his position that were not wounded. Kelsey wanted to establish a base of fire against the tree line. Sergeant Ackley hollered for two Marines to move towards the Lieutenant's position. Both Marines got up and took off running. The Marine in the lead made it ten yards before being struck by a hail of bullets, he collapsed into the paddy. The second Marine only made it five yards before he too was cut down by the withering fire. Sergeant Ackley and Lance Corporal Sheehy saw no movement from the first Marine. The second cried out that he had been shot through the shoulder and needed help.

Sergeant Ackley crawled over to the second Marine and told him to lie still. He had been hit twice, once in the stomach and once in the arm. Going into shock, he kept saying over and over again, "My stomach is on fire!"

To which Sergeant Ackley replied, "I'm sorry. There is nothing I can do. The Corpsman has been shot, hold on as long as you can."

Word was passed down the assault line for Sergeant Ackley to move to the Lieutenant's position with his Radioman. Lieutenant Kelsey's Radioman, Lance Corporal Deasel, had been shot and his radio damaged beyond use.

Sergeant Ackley slightly lifted his head from the cover of the paddy dike, scanning to his left, trying to locate Lieutenant Kelsey's position. No sooner did he raise his head when a bullet shattered through his neck while another hit him in the back of the head. He was killed instantly. It was his last day of his 18-month tour.

Lance Corporal Sheehy looking to his left, knew the approximate location of Lieutenant Kelsey. He knew the move to his location was tantamount to suicide, but the order had been given. He must get the radio to Lieutenant Kelsey. When Sheehy got to his feet he was already moving at a dead run. Moving like a half back towards the scrimmage line with the ball. His adrenaline was pumping so hard that he never felt the weight of the 25-pound radio or the 60 pounds of rifle and gear that he was carrying. As he sprinted all out through the rice paddy, he wondered how long before he would feel an NVA bullet tear through his body. He wondered how long he should run before he hit the ground, what angle he should take to further his movement towards the Lieutenant.

To his surprise he made it, dropping both body and gear close to the rice paddy dike. He felt he had just won the race of his life even though he knew it was only a momentary victory.

As Lance Corporal Sheehy turned his head looking at the Lieutenant, he noticed that he was lying next to a blood covered and apparently dead Marine. Turning he asked another Marine to his right, "Is he dead?"

In a near panic voice, the Marine stated, "Don't worry about it, he's ok. Just get the radio over here."

At the same time, another Marine further back in the paddy hollered towards the Lieutenant, "Sergeant Ackley just got shot in the head!"

Corporal Barnes, lying next to Lieutenant Kelsey, heard the words that Ackley was dead. It struck him hard, they were good friends, fighting alongside one another for many months. You could hear Marines every few minutes shouting out another name of a dead Marine. Corporal Barnes could hear Marines up and down the assault line cussing out their rifles as they continuously attempted to clear the jammed cartridges.

Staff Sergeant Tony Marengo would later state, "It was like fighting the enemy with muskets as we rammed our cleaning rods down our barrels to clear the jammed cartridges."

Many of the Marines on the battlefield were carrying their cleaning rods assembled and stuck in the back of their packs. Marines along the paddy dikes would lay on their backs and ram their cleaning rods down the barrel of their rifles to clear the jammed round from the chamber. They could only fire one round before having to clear the rifle again.

The enemy was effectively knocking out both leadership and communications throughout the battlefield and any attempt to move was suicidal.

The Third Platoon was still near the base of Hill A, behind Second Platoon. Corporal "Water Bu" Haley watched the Marines of Second Platoon being cut down and knew he had to do something. He crawled up to the first rice paddy dike. He could see and hear his ammo humper PFC Cliff Nolan, calling out. Haley shouted, "Get your ass over here!" When Nolan reached Haley, Staff Sergeant Marengo hollered for them to join him. Marengo had a grazing wound, but was still very much in charge.

The three Marines could hear Doc Martin shouting at two wounded Third Platoon machine gunners. He was crawling towards them to administer first aid. Suddenly Doc Martin shouted out, "I'm hit!"

Haley yelled, "Stay there! I'll get you!"

Martin countered, "No, don't! You'll get hit, I'll crawl to you."

Haley waited two minutes. The firing never stopped. "Doc, you okay?" Haley shouted. An answer never came. Sticking his head over the dike, he spotted Martin, dead, lying in the rice paddy. "Dammit Doc, why didn't you let me come." He lamented to himself.

Marengo ordered his Third Platoon to back out of the rice paddy into the base of Hill A. The move would protect them from the heavy fire being directed on top of them from Hill A. From there, they were hoping to be able to return fire to alleviate pressure on the other two platoons.

From out of nowhere, Captain Graham and his runner dove into the Third Platoons CP area. "How is your arm Tony?"

"It's fine Skipper. How is your shoulder?" Marengo asked, noting the Captain's bloody arm.

"I'm fine Tony. I want Corporal Long's Squad to get behind Hill A and silence that machine gun up there, it's killing my Second Platoon," Graham ordered. "He will have to circle to the south before advancing up. Alpha Company is moving to the junction of Hill A and B. The battalion command group and 81's are already on Hill B.

Shaking his head affirmatively, Marengo replied, "Aye, Aye."

Corporal Long had one of the best reputations for getting the job done. His tactical skills were superb and his fearless demeanor inspired his squad to the point of believing they were invincible.

"I need another squad to accompany me back. We need to start getting the casualties out of that rice paddy." Graham stated. "Corporal Nutt," who waved his hand towards Graham, "Go with the skipper to help with the casualties, take as many ponchos as you can find, you're gonna need them. Haley, send someone to get Long."

"Got it," nodded Haley. At the next break in firing, Graham, his runner and Nutt's Squad took off for the center of the battlefield near the base of Hill B.

Gunnery Sergeant Green motioned for Nutt's Squad to start evacuating First Platoon's wounded.

"Doc! you tell me who to carry out first," Corporal Nutt cried out to Hospital man, Third Class Wojda.

Pointing, Wodja yelled to Anderson, Groch, Lindstrom and Rizzo, "You guys! Work with Corporal Hester, he's got the whole thing organized."

It took Corporal Long's squad at least an hour to get to the southside of Hill A and begin their ascent up the side. While moving forward, automatic weapons fire rang out from the top. The Marines killed at least six enemy soldiers during their ascent. Every man in the squad sustained at least one wound. Once arriving near the top, the men started setting up a hasty defensive position. Lance Corporal Patrick Haley moved up with Long's Squad during the ascent. Long quickly spotted a machine gun emplacement that was firing down on the Second Platoon, further down the forward slope. Haley fired three rounds from his rocket launcher into the area where he thought the gun emplacements we're located. Within seconds, shrapnel hit his rocket launcher near the muzzle, rendering it inoperable.

Haley watched Corporal Long standing on a rock outcropping atop Hill A. He was firing his automatic weapon down into one of the NVA machine gun emplacements. Long was an unbelievable sight to see. This huge black Marine, no helmet, silhouetted against the top of the hill, making himself an obvious target to save the lives of his fellow Marines. It was a beautiful sight to behold. Long was psyched up, he was on a roll. Ignoring his wounds, he continued firing his weapon, inserting new magazines two or three times. He was like a wind whipped flame, unquenchable. Corporal Long had located the gun emplacements by listening for the sounds of the firing.

Corporal Melvin Long would receive The Navy Cross for his actions on the battlefield that day. After high school, Mel Long was drafted into the Marine Corps. He served a two-year hitch in the Corps before enrolling in college at the University of Toledo. He left college with the reputation of being the greatest lineman in the history of the Mid-American Conference. Toledo led the nation in defensive statistics the entire time Melvin Long played. He was inducted into the College Football Hall of Fame. Mel Long went on to play defensive tackle for three years with the Cleveland Browns. To Mel Long's friends and the Marines he served with, it wasn't his accomplishments on the gridiron, but the bravery and courage he showed on the battlefield in the jungles of Vietnam that made him a true American hero.

CPL Melvin Long with his dog Max, at his home in Toledo, OH

At the second gun emplacement, the NVA had dug tunnels and trenches permitting them to move their weapons to any of three, very well concealed, firing positions on the forward slope. It was obvious that considerable time had been spent before the battle preparing the tunneling, trenching, camouflaging and concealment in the area.

As Patrick Haley lay on the top of Hill A, only 19 years of age, his mind wandered through the godforsaken jungle; soldiers were trying to kill him. It was like a bad dream, it could not be happening, but it was. Why, oh why was it happening to him?

He would have his answer many years later when he saw the movie "Zulu" where the young British soldier turns to the detachment Sergeant Major and asks, "Why does it have to be us, Sergeant Major, why does it have to be us?"

To which the much traveled and decorated soldier calmly replied, "Because we are here, lad, because we are here!"

Lance Corporal Perry Jones, a machine gun team leader with Corporal Long's Squad could see Second Platoon in the rice paddy from where he was located. He was watching the Marines get annihilated by the machine guns to the front and the enemy soldiers in the bamboo tree line and spider traps to their left flank. He was devastated, he felt helpless because there was nothing he could do. He knew there were good friends of his in Second Platoon being demolished; Marines he had fought alongside for months.

Staff Sergeant Marengo had taken seven men and fought their way up Hill A from the left flank of Corporal Long's squad. Long's actions had diverted the enemy's attention, enabling Marengo to reach the top. Once reaching the top, Marengo and his men killed four enemy soldiers in a defensive position. It appeared the soldiers had been relaying information to their Commanders by the radio they had alongside them. They almost looked like Marines, except for their stature and Asian appearance. They had high and tight haircuts, fresh uniforms with brand new hi-top black sneakers. Some of the soldiers had camo uniforms and what we called black PJs, in their backpacks. Many of their AK-47's appeared to be new. They could certainly see these guys were regular NVA, fresh troops that just came down from the north.

The two machine guns to the front continued to rain down a blanket of devastating fire power. There was little Second Lieutenant Kelsey could do to either aid his men or lead a counterattack. Corporal Rick Barnes and Lance Corporal Jerry Westphal's fire team was on the far-left flank with McDonald's squad pinned down. The devastating machine gun fire to their front made it impossible to move or assault the gun emplacement. A heavy volume of fire coming from the bamboo tree line to their immediate left and the lethal trajectory of fire coming from the well-fortified position to the front, was killing or wounding anyone that moved. Second Platoon Marines who were deep inside the jaws of the ambush were dying from any slight movement, hell, they were dying when not moving.

1500 HOURS:

The battalion radio crackled to life, "Fox 6, this is a Millbrook 6, over." Lieutenant Colonel Hilgartner radioed for Graham.

Mackinnon answered, "Millbrook 6, this is Fox, over."

"Roger Fox, is Fox 6 available? Over."

"Fox Six is organizing an assault group from the remnants of Fox Two and the Charlie Papa group," Mackinnon explained.

"Roger, Fox, keep me informed, out."

1515 HOURS:

Lieutenant Kelsey, to the left of Barnes, slightly rose on one knee from the paddy and hollered to Lance Corporal Westphal. "Take your fire team and assault the machine gun position to your front! We've got to take it out, individual rushes!"

Corporal Barnes knew it was a suicide mission and watched as Westphal got up from the dike with both of his men along with Corporal McDonald and another Marine. Moving forward, within 30 feet, all five Marines were cut down by the weathering fire coming from the machine gun emplacement to the front. Three of the Marines clearly appeared to be beyond help, but Westphal was still moving. The machine gun continued to rake the 12" rice paddy dike with overwhelming fire. The rest of McDonald's squad held their ground, unable to move.

Corporal Barnes turned to Lance Corporal Gobrecht, "John, I'm going after Westphal, cover me."

Gobrecht replied, "Barnes you're married, I'll go."

Gobrecht, rising from the dike, started running towards the five Marines. Barnes got up and followed directly behind. Gobrecht grabbed Westphal's pack strap and Barnes got his leg, they dragged Westphal back to the shallow paddy dike from which they had just come.

Lying flat on the rice paddy behind the dike, Corporal Barnes cradled Westphal's head in his arms, he knew he was dying. Westphal was also married and a very close friend of Corporal Barnes. A bullet had entered the area of his left eye, exiting near his ear. Barnes held onto Westphal's head while his breathing became ragged; remaining with his brother until he took his last breath.

Corporal Barnes, still cradling Westphal's head, turned to Gobrecht while looking over at O'Brien, "I'm not lying here in this rice paddy and dying," pointing with his bloodied right hand, "I will die trying to take out that machine gun."

Gobrecht turned to his machine gunner PFC Mills while grabbing the machine gun, "I'm taking the gun and going with Barnes. You stay here and wait for more ammo. We only have one bandolier left."

Nothing motivated Marines more this day than to see their fellow Marines advancing towards the enemy and their objective.

Dahnawa— Cherokee for Warrior—translated, they run to the place of war.

Barnes along with Gobrecht and O'Brien got up out of the bloody water and led an assault on the tree line to their front. Muzzle flashes from enemy AK-47's and the rapid firing of a .51 Caliber machine gun were laying down destructive fire.

They ran 200 yards, zigzagging and screaming to reach the edge of the trenches where the enemy machine gun was located. They continuously fired into the enemy soldiers, who were being cut down by the bullets from the three Marines. Barnes, seeing a soldier attempting to get back on the machine gun, shot him before he could even turn it towards their direction. They fired into the soldiers crawling from the trenches attempting to escape. When reaching the trenches, Corporal Barnes' rifle jammed. Jumping into the trenches he picked up an AK-47 from one of the dead enemy soldiers. He continued firing at the NVA that decided to fight and into the backs of the retreating enemy. During the assault, it was as though a protective shield had been placed in front of all three Marines. Bullets were flying to the front and on all sides.

The three Marines could not be stopped. Barnes would kill more of the enemy that day with their own weapons than the Marine Corps issued M-16 rifle. He could feel blood running down the calf of his right leg into his boot. Still able to move, he did not stop to check the wound.

Lance corporal John Gobrecht ran through the tree line firing the M-60 at the retreating soldiers. He was soon out of ammo, grabbing three grenades one at a time, he threw them towards the soldiers. John, realizing he was out of ammo, stopped dead in his tracks, spotting two camouflaged enemy soldiers in the bush. They both carried AK-47 assault rifles. All three stood, transfixed on one another, not moving a muscle. Realizing he had no more ammo in his machine gun he thought he would be shot at any moment. Both NVA soldiers silently disappeared into the foliage. What was left of the enemy had fled into the tree line to their south. The three Marines immediately saw freshly dug fighting holes and tunnel entrances. They seemed to be everywhere.

Lieutenant Kelsey, after seeing Barnes and the two Marines assaulting the machine gun position, got up from the paddy with his Radioman Lance Corporal Sheehy. The two got within 50 yards of the tree line ducking down behind a rice paddy dike.

Looking over at the Lieutenant, Sheehy could see him attempting to unjam his M-16 rifle. As soon as Sheehy looked back a bullet smashed through his right arm, between the elbow and his shoulder. At first, he was not aware that he had been hit, not until he felt the overwhelming pain in his arm. He felt a steady stream of blood running down his chest. Realizing his arm lay across his back, he attempted to pull his arm back to the front of his chest. He could feel the bone fragments tearing at his flesh as he attempted to pull his arm around.

Lieutenant Kelsey crawled over to Sheehy, seeing that he had been hit. He took the field dressing from his first aid pouch and wrapped it around Sheehy's shattered arm. The Lieutenant then took his own web belt off and wrapped it around the field dressing, putting pressure on the wound to stop most of the bleeding. Sheehy's rifle had flung 10 feet in front of the rice paddy dike when he was hit. Without saying a word, Second Lieutenant Kelsey got up from the dike, continuing his assault towards the tree line, retrieving Sheehy's rifle as he ran.

Suddenly Sheehy heard his call sign over the radio, it was Mac McKinnon, the command group Radioman. Sheehy had forgotten that the radio was still strapped to his back. "Fox 3, this is Fox 6, Over."

Reaching for his handset, Sheehy quickly replied, "Fox 6 this is Fox 3."

"Fox 3, get the Lieutenant on the radio."

"The Lieutenant is not here, I'm wounded bad."

"Fox 3, repeat coordinates given earlier for airstrike on NVA position to your front."

"Fox 6, I have not seen the Lieutenant since he entered the tree line, do not know coordinates," the radio went silent.

Corporal Karl Rische saw Lieutenant Kelsey assaulting the tree line. He witnessed Kelsey's Radioman being shot. Getting up from the paddy, he ran to Sheehy's position. He saw Sheehy was severely wounded. Rische pulled the radio off of Sheehy, slipped into the radio pack harness himself, got up and continued towards the tree line.

L/CPL Dennis Sheehy

1535 HOURS:

To the far-right flank of Second Platoon, Captain Graham was leading an assault with his Radioman Corporal Dirickson, Gunnery Sergeant Green, Lance Corporal Painter, Lance Corporal Mike Discoll, PFC Tom LaBarbera, PFC Jack Milton, Corporal John Francis and the Company Corpsman Petty Officer Donovan. Green took the front of the charge, killing 10 NVA himself during the assault.

Gunnery Sergeant Green would receive the Navy Cross for his assault on the tree line.

They came in on the right side of the bombed out French built house.

Corporal Barnes, along with Gobrecht and O'Brien, had come in on the far-left side of the bombed out French house and the defensive position during their assault. Lieutenant Kelsey and Corporal Karl Rische, with four or five more Marines from Rische's Squad, followed behind Barnes.

Corporal Barnes and Gunnery Sergeant Green organized the able and wounded men forming a hasty defensive position. They had gone without water since noon. Gunny Green knew he couldn't do anything about the dehydration but both he and Barnes re-distributed what little ammunition was left. 18 Marines had made it to the tree line. Most were glad just to still be alive.

ROARING FLAMES IN THE DARKNESS

"Everyone is a moon and has a dark side which he never shows to anybody."

-Mark Twain

8.1 *Desperate Fight for Survival*

1545 HOURS:

18 Marines got up out of the rice paddy knowing that whatever they did would probably get them killed. They would take the tree line and a piece of Objective Foxtrot.

Ordinary men did extraordinary things that day in the rice paddies. So many courageous men, putting their lives on the line to help their wounded comrades; heroic acts occurred simultaneously all over that battlefield. Most of the survivors of Fox Company had no idea what their brothers in arms went through until after the war was over or they encountered one another in hospitals; rejoicing in the fact that a friend made it through and saddened to learn that other friends did not. Hearing the stories, reliving the moments, willingly or not...

Corporal Barnes scanned the tree line they had just taken. It was an island containing an old bombed out French house. The four standing walls varied from three to four feet in height. To the east of the island was a 100 m wide rice paddy, separating the beginning of the Vinh Huy 2, Village. To the south was a thick bamboo wall of vegetation. Barnes could see enemy movement throughout the brush line. To the north was 400 m of open rice paddy towards the Village of Chau Lam. As he looked back towards the rice paddy from which he had just come, it was littered with dead and wounded Marines from Second Platoon.

Barnes ran over to the entrance to the French house where a dead Marine lay. Throwing down the AK-47, containing an empty magazine, he picked up an M-16 rifle next to the Marine's body. Checking the chamber to see if the cartridge cleared, Barnes reached for the canteen on the Marine's web belt for water, it was empty. He then removed a grenade from the dead Marine, placing it in his lower right fatigue pocket.

Corporal Barnes and Gunnery Sergeant Green organized the Marines along with the wounded men and formed a hasty defensive position. In the sweltering heat, they had gone without water since before noon. Everyone knew nothing could be done about the dehydration. With little ammunition left, the Marines redistributed what they had amongst one another. Corporal Barnes picked up another AK-47 with a full magazine, laying it alongside his fighting position to the south.

Captain Graham was leaning against the northeast corner of the bombed out French house. The Captain had Corporal Dirickson's radio slung over his right shoulder. Graham had been shot earlier through the left arm and hit again during the assault on the tree line. Corporal Dirickson had been shot through the stomach and was lying next to the Captain; he was paralyzed from the waist down with a severed spinal cord. The Company Corpsman, Doc Donovan, was administering first aid.

Finally making contact with Lieutenant Colonel Hilgartner, Graham announced that he had taken a portion of Objective Foxtrot.

First Sergeant Lee had remained on the other side of the rice paddy where a Fox Company command post had been set up. Wounded Marines from First Platoon we're being evacuated to that location. Captain Graham was able to contact Lee advising him to send any available Marines and ammunition to his location.

Second Lieutenant Kelsey came up to Corporal Barnes on the south end of the tree line with PFC LaBarbera and CPL Painter.

"Barnes, give me two men. I'm going to circle that machine gun pounding us from that tree line," pointing across the rice paddy towards Vinh Huy 2."

"Francis, you and Butler go with the lieutenant," Barnes ordered as he pointed to the tree line in front of him to the south, "that tree line is full of NVA. We need to hold this line, we've got dead and wounded already."

Kelsey replied, "Barnes, I've been ordered to take out that gun, you've got to hold this line."

Barnes, looked back at Kelsey, "Good luck."

Corporal Barnes moved over to the left side of the French house, positioning himself towards the west and Vinh Huy 2. He wanted to be in a location that could give covering fire for Lieutenant Kelsey and his group of Marines.

John Gobrecht crawled over alongside Barnes, holding an old concrete pot with stagnant water in it, "Here Barnes, I found some water," as he handed the pot to Barnes.

"Thanks John." It was hot, filthy stuff, but it tasted good.

Corporal Barnes had been in country for over 15 months. He had been in many fire fights and ambushes and this one had seemed to be no different. Now realizing they had walked into a hornet's nest, it was time to go on the defense. They needed to hold their ground and get the wounded and dead off the battlefield.

Lieutenant Kelsey and his assault group traversed safely on the rice paddy side of the island to its south end. From there, they hovered nearly 20 m away from the Vinh Huy hamlet's true tree line. The Lieutenant charged first as Francis, Painter and LaBarbera stayed with him. A sniper round hit Kelsey as he entered the tree line. Kelsey's body toppled forward halfway through the bamboo thicket. Francis, Painter and LaBarbera hit the ground 15 feet in front of Kelsey.

Francis got to his knees, yelling to the rest of the men, "Spread out!" waving his arms in a gesture to back up his command.

A round seared through his forehead, halting any further movement; leaving a deep crimson hole with blood splatter across his face. Only Painter and LaBarbera, the two admin clerks, along with PFC Butler, remained in the group.

Moments later, Painter was also struck by a bullet through the head. Corporal Barnes lay in a small opening alongside the French house. He watched one of the Marines from Kelsey's group running from the Vinh Huy Village tree line towards his position. The Marine ran with his knees reaching for the sky as he raced towards the safety of the tree line island. Barnes watched as the Marine ran across the paddy and landed in the opening, falling right next to Barnes.

Looking up at the Marine, Barnes asked, "Butler, where the fuck is your rifle?"

The Marine stated in a panicked voice, "There's hundreds of them on the other side of that tree line. The Lieutenant is dead and everybody else."

Barnes replied, "Find yourself a rifle, there's plenty of them laying around."

Barnes got up, moving over to Lance Corporal Gobrecht and Corporal O'Brien, "John, Obie, it's not good. Lieutenant Kelsey is dead and there's hundreds of NVA on the other side of that Paddy," pointing to the west, "Where's your M-60 John?"

"It's laying over there Barnes. There's no more bandoliers."

"Bring it to me John." Corporal Barnes started dismantling the machine gun, throwing the parts in different directions. "I don't know if we're gonna get out of here John, they're not gonna get our machine gun."

First Sergeant Lee radioed back to Graham and relayed the news that the five men he sent from the company headquarters had only made it halfway across the rice paddy before they were cut down. The ammo was almost gone.

Corporal Barnes, Gobrecht and O'Brien were now defending the south side of the island. NVA soldiers were firing from the bamboo tree line and periodically running out towards the three Marines. The fighting was now taking place 30 to 40 feet from their position. Gobrecht and O'Brien were in front of an old house bunker to the right of Barnes.

Barnes took aim as he saw an NVA soldier running directly towards him. Barnes had risen into a standing position. A B40, RPG round (rocket propelled grenade) came flying out of the tree line, landing in front of Lance Corporal Gobrecht. Barnes' rifle flew five feet into the air as the grenade exploded. His arms were still extended to his front, as if he was holding the rifle. He felt the bones snap in both arms; blood began to gush out of his left arm and more spurted out with each beat of his heart.

There was no question both of his arms were broken in multiple places. The explosion was deafening. Pieces of red, hot metal had gone into his hip, side, and his head, with some entering his right ear as well.

Falling to the ground, Barnes, with two broken arms, could do nothing but watch the blood pumping out of his body. He was still bleeding from an earlier wound to his upper, right calf muscle and his upper, right arm. The enemy soldier he had aimed for lay dead, 15 feet in front of him, hit by his own comrade's RPG round.

Gobrecht's jaw had been ripped apart and metal was buried deep inside his thigh muscles. Corporal O'Brien had a metal shard sticking out of his neck. O'Brien, still able to talk, hollered for Corpsman Doc Donovan, "Gobrecht's been hit!" not realizing his own wounds.

Barnes crawled over to Donovan, with blood gushing from his wounds, "Doc you've got to put a tourniquet on this arm before I bleed out."

Donovan, cutting off Barnes' pack straps, removed his web belt. Donovan had long since run out of morphine. Ripping open his jungle fatigue shirt, he had some battle dressings left but supplies were depleting rapidly. Donovan put dressings on both arms, pulling the strings tight in an attempt to stop the bleeding. "Barnes, I can't do anything further. I'm running out of dressings. I've got wounded all over the place, I have to go."

While giving aid to John Gobrecht, John handed his diary to Doc Donovan and asked, "Doc, make sure it gets back to my family." He had maintained a diary since arriving in Vietnam. Realizing he was close to death, he did not want the enemy to get their hands on it.

Two Marines moved the three wounded alongside Captain Graham and Corporal Dirickson before taking defensive positions back on the south end.

Corporal Barnes lay to the right side of Captain Graham, at his feet. To the right of Barnes was Corporal Dirickson, paralyzed from the waist down with a wound to his lower chest. Behind Barnes and leaning against the backside of the north wall of the French house, was Gobrecht and O'Brien.

184

Barnes could hear every word the Captain was saying. He had a clear view north, across the rice paddy towards Chau Lam and Delta Company's location.

There were two F-4 Phantom Jets circling above. He could see three assault lines of NVA soldiers about 200 m to his front. The soldiers had jungle foliage tied to their backs and helmets. Every time an F-4 Phantom would make a pass the enemy would get down as if to disappear.

Barnes saw the Marines from Delta Company coming out of the tree line approximately 400 m to his front, moving towards Chau Lam.

He saw the smoke from the gunfire and explosions from grenades, RPGs and Delta's 81 mortars. For a short, few minutes, there was a feeling that help was coming and survival might be possible. That quickly faded away as he watched Delta Company get pushed back into the tree line from which they came. Now, the feeling of death, imminent.

Delta Company's First Platoon Commander, Lt Chmiel and Platoon Sergeant, S/Sgt Dixon had already been killed. Cpl Barnes was witnessing Lt Bill Links' Third Platoon attempting to come in on the enemy's left flank to relieve the pressure on Delta's First and Second Platoons. Lt. Links' effort was valiant, but unsuccessful as they were soon pushed back into the tree line after coming under heavy enemy fire. Help was not on its way. The cavalry was not coming.

Colonel Hilgartner's Alpha Company was approximately 1000 m to the rear of Fox Company's position on Hills A and B. They were completely out of sight due to heavy jungle foliage. Captain Babich led his company into terrain covered with extremely high brush which made it impossible for the attacking Marines to see the concealed enemy. Unknown to Fox Company, well over a platoon of NVA had moved into their rear and sealed them off from Alpha Company's advance. Alpha's first contact with the concealed enemy was when their Third Platoons' point fire team encountered a lone enemy soldier hidden in a large rock crevice. The Marine on point was immediately shot. The enemy soldier tried to drag the wounded Marine to his hiding place. When the Marine yelled for help, the enemy soldier shot two additional Marines coming to his aid. The remainder of the squad took cover.

Captain Babich came on scene and began organizing his Marines for an attack. During the assault on the enemy position, in an attempt to retrieve his dead and wounded Marines, Captain Babich was killed.

During this engagement a machine gun team from Alpha Company had gotten lost and separated from the company. Staff Sergeant Marengo's Third Platoon Fox Company Commander ran across the gun team while moving his men off of Hill A. The gun team advised Marengo that Alpha was just behind them. Alpha Company never came. With Captain Babich dead they had been ordered to re-enforce the First Battalion Headquarters area. The reserve Company was not coming to get us out. No one was.

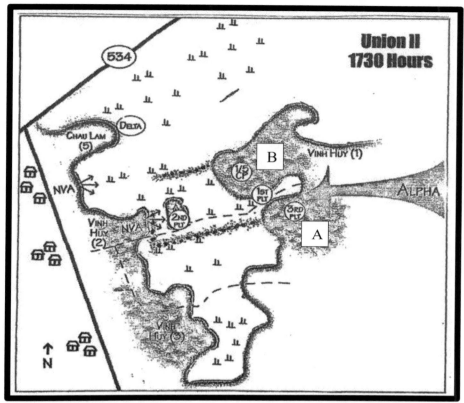

*Photo Courtesy of "Battlelines" by LtCol David Brown

1730 HOURS:

Gunnery Sergeant Green stood in front of Captain Graham with four Marines still standing and in the fight. The battle in the tree line had evolved to a point with only a handful of Marines left and no ammunition remaining; a decision had to be made. Barnes listened as Graham gave an order, "Gunny, take your four men and get over to Third Platoon's area as quickly as possible."

With this, Barnes turned to Gobrecht and O'Brien, thinking they were leaving. Before he could utter the words, *we are getting out of here*, Barnes turned back and Gunny Green and the four Marines were gone. Gunny Green, PFC Tom LaBarbera and the other three Marines must not have realized that Corporal Barnes, laying at the Captain's feet, was still alive. Bleeding from multiple wounds he likely appeared to be dead or dying. Corporal O'Brien and L/Cpl Gobrecht were both lying at the backside of the French house wall, behind Captain Graham. They were not visible to the five Marines or the Captain.

1745 HOURS:

Captain Graham called to Lieutenant Colonel Hilgartner, "Millbrook six, this is Fox six, over."

Hilgartner must have been waiting for the call. He answered directly, "Roger, Jim, what's your situation?"

"I've moved as many of my men back to the rear as I can. I'm here with my wounded we're probably not going to make it. I'm out of ammo and I've got NVA making an assault on my position."

"Jim, I have no troops available to send your way, can you get out on your own?"

"Millbrook 6, I will not leave any of my wounded or dead behind."

The silence mounted as Hilgartner stared mutely at the radio. He would not hear from Captain Graham again.

"Fox three, this is Fox six, over," Graham called for Staff Sergeant Marengo.

"Roger six, go."

Marengo responded within moments, "Tony, can you help me?"

Marengo shook his head as though Graham could see him. "Skipper, I just arrived at high ground behind Hill A. I am consolidating what's left of the company. We have one squad and they are assisting the wounded in establishing the defensive position," Marengo turned to his radio operator with a look of helplessness, "There's nothing we can do." Marengo pressed the button on the handset once more, "We recommend you stay where you are, Skipper. I've been in contact with Alpha Company and I'm going to send them to your position. They should be up there soon."

"It's a little bit late for that," came Graham's solemn response. His voice took on the commanding tone it normally held, "You stay where you are Tony. They are firing and maneuvering against me and they look pretty good—"

Graham's last transmission broke off; the radio fell silent. Tony still did not think the Captain was actually being overrun. He knew the Captain needed help but did not realize the situation had become so dire.

Captain Graham turned to the Company Corpsman, Petty Officer Thomas Donovan, "Doc, you've got to get out of here!"

"Captain, I can't leave, it's my duty. I have wounded Marines laying here."

Lieutenant Kelsey was dead and Captain Graham was shot through the left shoulder, with an additional leg wound. The NVA was closing in with every passing second. Captain Graham was partially standing against the short wall of the French house, the radio slung over his right shoulder as he spoke into the handset. The Captain's rifle was leaning against his right leg alongside his pistol which was holstered to his leg.

Corporal Barnes could hear every word Captain Graham and the Phantom Jet pilot said as he circled overhead.

"Fox 6, this is Sky Ryder, over."

"We copy Sky Ryder, how does it look from above?"

"Not good Fox 6. I see several hundred NVA advancing to assault your position."

"How long do we have?"

"Fox 6 you are about to be overrun."

"When they get on top...drop your heat."

"Did you say *on top* Fox 6?"

"Affirmative Sky Ryder. I say again to confirm, drop your heat on top of our position; I say again, when we are overrun, drop on top."

As a wounded 19-year-old, Corporal Rick Barnes thought this was where he was going to die. There was no way out. He listened to the Fox Company Commander's conversation with two, fast-moving fighter jets above a rice paddy in Vietnam. He couldn't believe how desperate the battle had become and that over 150 U.S. Marines had already been killed or wounded. Barnes knew the battle was coming to a close with the enemy only 100 m away. Everything was happening so fast; the minutes were passing as seconds.

The enemy was now 40 m to the front. After fighting Major Dao Cong's Second Battalion in the initial assault on Objective Foxtrot, Barnes was now about to face another 500 enemy soldiers from the Third Battalion, 31st Regiment, moving in from the north. They were the same unit that had been fighting Delta Company to the right flank of Fox.

Corporal Barnes could see the face of the enemy soldiers and could hear the orders being passed in Vietnamese. The NVA soldiers were masters at camouflage. They would cover their helmets and backs with brush, blending into the environment like chameleons. The NVA would work in teams when applying camouflage, with each soldier carrying a wire or bamboo wooden frame on their backs that acted as a skeleton frame to attach the vegetation.

When one of the jets would fly overhead, they stopped, crouched down and remained motionless, practically invisible. Barnes watched as they used this tactic moving towards their position.

Corporal Dirickson was sitting upright, despite the fact he would never have use of his legs again. He leaned over the top of Barnes, tugging at Captain Graham's bloodied fatigues, "What do I do Captain?" Dirickson's voice was desperate, "I don't know what to do! I can't move my legs. I feel this god-awful pressure and I want to know what I should do."

With the enemy soldiers swiftly approaching and the Marine jets starting to make their run, Captain Graham picked up the rifle leaning against his leg and tossed it over Barnes, onto Dirickson's lap, "Do the best you can, Marine, they're coming."

1750 HOURS:

With no ammunition left, Captain Graham realized that we were about to be overrun and our hopeless fate was before us. He again, ordered Corpsman Donovan, who although wounded himself continued to take care of his Marines, "Try and get any of the remaining wounded back across the paddy." But by the time the order was given, it was too late. The enemy was within 20 yards of their position, advancing in rigid assault lines.

Barnes stuck his head around the corner of the house wall behind him, where Gobrecht and O'Brien were laying, "John, Obie, can you move? If we don't, we are going to die." Both Marines nodded their heads in affirmation. The three Marines crawled 20 feet and ducked behind the low wall at the south end of the French house.

Barnes leaned around the corner of the wall and watched Captain Graham firing his pistol point-blank into the oncoming enemy soldiers.

CPL Marion Dirickson

Corporal Dirickson was slamming his fist against his rifle as he hollered, "This fucking rifle!" Apparently, a casing was stuck in the chamber and it wouldn't function. Barnes listened as the enemy soldiers shouted orders.

He turned to John and Obie, "We've got to move again, John, let's go for the rice paddy, can you make it across the trench line?"

Nodding their heads in unison, the three Marines moved towards the trench line, now only 40 feet from the enemy.

Captain Graham and Corporal Dirickson were both dead.

The enemy had lined the front of the trench that was bordering the paddy with two lines of single, barbed wire. As the three Marines attempted to cross, Barnes and Gobrecht tripped on the wire. As Barnes was falling across the trench line, he looked to his right and saw an enemy soldier firing his AK-47 into Corporal O'Brien's back. Barnes and Gobrecht lay five feet in front of the trench line at the edge of the paddy, only six feet apart from one another. The Vietnamese were shouting commands directly behind them, sporadic gunfire could be heard, the roar of the F-4 Phantom jet coming in for its bomb run was overhead...

Suddenly Doc Donovan appeared to the right of Barnes, crawling a foot from his side. Barnes, with his head turned towards Donovan, saw an NVA Officer standing over them both. The Officer reached down with his pistol in hand and shot Donovan to the back of the head. Donovan's face dropped into the mud as Barnes watched the bullet pass through the back of his skull. Another enemy soldier came up on Barnes' left side, slamming his butt stock against Barnes' neck and head as the NVA Officer to his right, relentlessly kicked him in the ribs. Barnes could see another soldier standing over Gobrecht. Barnes tried to move his hand to his right fatigue pocket to remove the grenade he had strategically placed there earlier. Realizing he could not move his fingers on his broken right hand, he stopped, wondering if the soldiers standing over him noticed his movement. With two broken arms and several holes throughout his body, he was too close to death to fight. He waited for a bullet to the head. He knew the bullet was coming. He knew his fate was sealed.

Overhead he could still hear a Jet coming, most likely on its final run, ready to drop a 500-pound bomb on their position.

The Officer then put the gun to Barnes' head. Seconds before the trigger could be pulled, the roar of the jet passed directly overhead, with an immediate explosion 25 m from their location. The ground shook as Barnes could see the three soldiers disappearing with the blast, mud and smoldering, smoking earth, covered both Barnes and Gobrecht.

By late afternoon into evening, as Corporal Barnes and L/Cpl Gobrecht lay in front of the tree line, the F-4 Phantom jets began dropping their payloads in and behind the tree line. L/Cpl Sheehy and PFC Mike Hernandez lay in the rice paddy where the debris from the bomb blasts were landing all around them. Bamboo trees, dirt and vegetation were scattered throughout the paddy. At one point, what appeared to be the metal base plate of a mortar tube or part of one of the machine gun positions, came flying through the air. Unable to move, Sheehy thought it was going to strike him in the head. The metal plate just missed him, landing directly to his front. After one of the bomb runs, they could see bodies flying into the air. The Marines that were still alive in the rice paddy had no idea if they were enemy bodies or the Marines that had entered the tree line.

As the bomb runs continued, Corporal Barnes lost consciousness.

Captain Graham, with a small contingent of Marines from Second Platoon, had taken Objective Foxtrot. The Marines had held their position until confronted with overwhelming enemy numbers. Fighting with an M-16 rifle that had failed them and no ammunition remaining for their M-60 machine guns, the decision had been made to deny the enemy the hard-fought objective. Surrender was not an option. Airstrikes were called on top of their position. The ultimate sacrifice was made.

For sustained acts of heroism on June 2, Corporal Brent "Mac" Mackinnon received the Navy Commendation Medal with combat V. As the head Radioman for Captain James Graham, Corporal Mackinnon maintained vital radio communication throughout the battle. At one point during the afternoon, Captain Graham requested help for his Marines pinned down in the contested tree line. In a valiant effort, Corporal Mackinnon lead a five-man assault on Captain Graham's position. After receiving numerous casualties, Corporal Mackinnon was forced to abandon his gallant effort to relieve the pressure on the beleaguered Marines.

Corporal Tom McDonald came crawling back to where PFC Hernandez and the other two Marines were laying, "Mike, you guys follow me back to the base of Hill A."

One of the Marines asked McDonald about the other guy that had been shot when he attempted the assault on the machine gun earlier, "He's dead," McDonald replied.

Before they turned back towards Hill A, Mike Hernandez saw several NVA soldiers appear in the tree line where Barnes and Gobrecht were laying. One of the soldiers was holding one of our M-60 machine guns. Brown, a crack shot from Tennessee, was lying to the right of Hernandez. Brown yelled, "Let me shoot the son of a bitch first!" They promptly saw the enemy soldier drop.

Staying low, they found a depression on the left side of the hill and followed it along Hill A. Suddenly, a machine gun opened up from Hill A. They yelled, "We're Marines!"

"C'mon up" was the reply.

As darkness fell over the battlefield, the four Marines
reached the perimeter that the surviving Marines had set up.
Wounded and dead Marines were lying everywhere on top
of the hill. McDonald advised them to stay put. PFC
Hernandez crouched down next to the large boulder where
Yeutter had been shot that morning when the battle had
started. Word was passed along the perimeter that NVA
patrols were out in the rice paddy shooting our wounded
Marines.

PFC Mike Hernandez

For conspicuous gallantry and intrepidity, at the risk of his
life above and beyond the call of duty, Captain James

Graham was awarded the Medal of Honor; he was 26 years old.

One of Captain Graham's Company Radiomen, Corporal Brent "Mac" Mackinnon said it best, "Captain Jim Graham was courageous when the time came; not with guns blazing to assault and destroy, but in a doomed effort to save our people in the Second Platoon, ambushed in a rice paddy. He is an authentic hero, a caring person, who did the right thing at the right time and sacrificed himself in an impossible situation."

Petty officer Thomas Donovan was awarded a Silver Star, posthumously, for his heroic conduct, selfless courage, and resolute devotion to duty. Refusing to leave the battlefield when ordered, realizing it was his solemn duty to take care of his wounded Marines, knowing there was no chance for survival.

Staff Sergeant Tony Marengo had great admiration for Doc Tom Donovan, He started with Fox Company as a Corpsman for Tony's Third Platoon. Thinking he would be safer as head Corpsman for Headquarters Section, Tony authorized his transfer. Little did he realize what lay ahead. Being from Natick, Mass. Tony felt that he was not only a great Corpsman, but a truly good person. Tom Donovan would die on his birthday.

Corporal Rick Barnes for his courage, aggressive fighting spirit and steadfast devotion to duty in the face of extreme personal danger, would be awarded the Silver Star. Fox Company was suddenly subjected to mortar, small arms and automatic weapons fire from heavily fortified positions along tree lines bordering a large open rice paddy, temporarily pinning down lead elements of the Second Platoon and inflicting numerous casualties. Observing a wounded Marine lying in an exposed area, Corporal Barnes, with complete disregard for his own safety and without hesitation, advanced under heavy hostile fire to recover his fallen companion and move him to a protected area. He led one of his gun teams on the assault of a fortified machine gun position despite multiple wounds and continued on through heavy gunfire. Corporal Barnes and his men would overrun the position, securing a section of Objective Foxtrot.

L/CPL John Gobrecht

8.2 *The Night Escape*

Pray to be sheltered from danger but to be fearless in facing it.

1800 HOURS:

Darkness had fallen over the battlefield. The only sounds were the Vietnamese conversing, the moaning of the dying, and single gunshots echoing through the night as the enemy soldiers walked through the fallen Marines, ensuring every American was dead.

Staff Sergeant Marengo got First Sergeant Lee on the Company radio, "First Sergeant, I'm going after the Captain."

"Tony, he's dead," was Lee's response.

Marengo insisted, "Then I'm going after his body."

"Marengo, return to the CP. You can't help him, it's too late."

Gunnery Sergeant Green and Lance Corporal Mackinnon arrived at the Third Platoon's command post position. As the sky darkened, Staff Sergeant Marengo had left Corporal Long on Hill A, until the last chance of hope for Graham's survival and his rejoining the surviving Fox Marines had vanished. Corporal Long was moved back to higher ground, some 600 m behind Hill A. The new position was picked so medevacs could be maintained throughout the night. Gunny Green caught up with Marengo.

"Hey Tony, I need a squad to assist any of the wounded who might be able to make it."

Marengo, addressing Perry Jones said, "PJ, hook up with Conley, and see what you can do."

"Gotcha, Staff Sergeant, I'm on it now."

"Hey Gunny, did you see Corporal Barnes or Hanover, Gobrecht?" Jones asked.

"They were both wounded laying by the Skipper, I thought they were trying to get out when I left. That was 45 minutes ago." Green answered.

"We have to evacuate at least another 20 wounded. At this point, we have 17 bodies as well. I already evacuated 12 wounded after Long took Hill A," Marengo mentioned.

"Also, I want to get the whole company here before dark so we can circle the wagons before anything else happens," Green stated.

PFC Terry Klein, from Tony's Third Platoon, could hear Marines down in the rice paddy calling for help. On the edge of the rice paddy, at the bottom of Hill A, he could hear a Marine's voice that kept saying, "Kline, Kline, Gary Kline help me."

Terry knew there was another marine in the Second Platoon by the name of Gary Kline. Moving down to the bottom of the hill he crawled over and lay next to the badly wounded Marine. He held his hand until he was finally carried up for evacuation.

By mid-afternoon on June 2, Lieutenant Colonel Hilgartner realized his battalion was in a bad situation.

He contacted the Fifth Marine Regimental Commander, Colonel Houghton, advising him of the predicament. Since Colonel Houghton's Third Battalion was already involved in heavy fighting, he asked for the commitment of the division reserve, Lieutenant Colonel Jackson's Second Battalion, Fifth Marines.

Major general Donn Robertson, who had just assumed command of the Division on June 1, concurred and the Second Battalion prepared to move out by helicopter to join in the battle. The three companies that made up Lieutenant Colonel Jackson's Sparrow Hawk reactionary force for this operation were his own Echo Company, Company D from the First Battalion, Seventh Marines and Company E, Second Battalion, Seventh Marines.

The Fifth Marines' Commander paved the way for the Second Battalion's entry into the operation by ordering 90 minutes of air and artillery preparation for the planned landing zone. He inserted the battalion northeast of the enemy position, so it could drive south, into its left flank.

1900 HOURS:

The two companies had landed. They were just north, on Route 534 at its junction with the dirt road to Chau Lam (5) which had been Delta 1/5's Objective.

Landing after Echo Company 2/5 was part of 2/5's Command Group and Delta 1/7. They were unopposed and quickly organized the position.

As night fell, one of Jackson's companies, Echo Company from Second Battalion, Seventh Marines, still had not arrived. Aware of the urgency of the situation facing Hilgartner's Battalion and rising concern for the fate of Captain Graham's company from his own battalion, Lieutenant Colonel Jackson requested permission to begin his attack without the missing company. The command group and Colonel Houghton concurred.

Leaving a security platoon in the landing zone, Jackson put his S-3 officer, Major Dick Esau, in charge. Esau maneuvered his force south against the enemy. The battalion had not gone far into the darkness before Echo Company collided with the

NVA force that had assaulted and overrun Captain Graham's position. Catching the enemy by surprise, the Marines quickly drove through their position and continued south. The move by Major Dick Esau, attacking in the dark of the night in unfamiliar territory, saved the day for the remaining troops of Fox Company and the First Battalion. It certainly prevented a counterattack during the night by the enemy troops.

The Marines suffered almost 20 casualties in the initial contact and called in a passing CH-53. The pilot landed the helicopter in the middle of the command post, not far from where Echo Company was still engaged with the enemy. As Marines completed loading the wounded, an enemy mortar round landed just to the rear of the aircraft, enemy automatic weapons took it under direct fire. The pilot quickly took off. The Second Battalion would hear later that on its arrival in Da Nang, the ground crew counted 58 holes in the helicopter.

The sudden presence of a strong force on its northern flank caused the NVA units to disengage and make a hasty withdrawal to the southwest, but the move proved costly. Once the enemy soldiers left the protection of their fortifications, they were easy targets for Marines supporting arms fire. The airstrikes were devastating. On one occasion 2, F-4 aircrafts used an unusual technique of target acquisition which proved especially effective. The first aircraft approached the area at low speed and switched on its landing and running lights. When the enemy fired at the plane, the second aircraft, following closely behind without lights, spotted the enemy and dropped napalm on the firing positions. The medevac helicopters often used the same tactic to get their choppers in during a heavy fire fight. The first helicopter would draw the enemy fire while the second landed and executed the medevac.

You could always tell which aircrafts were piloted by the Marines...the ones with the elephant grass in the bomb racks and the helicopters full of bullet holes.

Corporal Barnes must have appeared lifeless to the NVA Soldiers walking among the dead Marines. The blood from his multiple wounds was so severe, that he appeared to be lying in a pool of it, completely red, soaked paddy water. Gobrecht must have also seemed to be beyond the price of a bullet as brutal facial and leg wounds allowed him to pass for the dead.

2100 HOURS:

When Corporal Barnes regained consciousness on the battlefield, it was pitch black. The sounds of war were ringing in his ears. Doc Donovan's dead body was still lying to his right. Slightly raising his head to look over the top of Donovan, he could see John Gobrecht. It took all his energy to whisper, "John are you OK?"

"I'm still here, Barnes," came the response, "Have you seen any movement from Obie?"

"No, he's dead."

Barnes knew that death squads would be moving through the rice paddies during the night, removing their dead before morning. His immediate concern was that if they find one of them, they'll find both of them since they were lying only a few feet from the enemy trenches they had assaulted just hours earlier.

To help their odds of survival, Barnes attempted to raise his head again and whispered to Gobrecht, "We need to separate. You move towards the right and I will go left."

Gobrecht slightly raised his left hand inches off the ground and gave Barnes a thumbs up. He watched Gobrecht move to the right, front of his position until he lost sight of him in the darkness. Barnes had lost a lot of blood and was going in and out of consciousness at this point. He lay there waiting for a bullet to the back of the head.

His biggest fear was the thought of being captured. He remembered all the stories the instructors would tell them while they were going through jungle warfare school and why you would want to avoid capture at all cost. He still wondered how he could get the grenade out of his fatigue pocket and pull the pin if capture was unavoidable. He tried to crawl to his left front. The pain when dragging his arms in the mud filled rice paddy was unbearable. After moving a short ten yards, he stopped. He could see movement to his right flank along the bamboo tree line and to his rear. Periodic flares would go off in the far distance casting a dim light over the battlefield. He could tell they were enemy soldiers. They appeared to have some type of hook they were using to drag they're dead. A rope with a grappling iron tied to one end was used by the NVA to hook bodies and drag a distance away to be buried in shallow graves.

Barnes heard a Marine a short distance to his left, pleading, "help me, help me." Barnes wanted to holler at him to shut up, but knew he couldn't. A short time later, right before he passed out again, a single shot rang out nearby and the voice went silent.

In front of Barnes and to the left about 20 yards, behind a paddy dike, lay PFC Sheehy. He was in tremendous pain from his arm being shattered by a 51-caliber bullet. It felt like his arm was on fire. He reached over with his good hand, touching his wounded arm. It was then that he realized his arm was covered with fire ants. The blood dripping from his arm had attracted them. The red ants were common in Vietnam; he had been bitten by them before and it wasn't pleasant.

Looking up, he heard the roar of jet engines. He could see a jet approaching with what appeared to be his wing landing lights on. A second jet appeared. As the Jets passed overhead, he could see fire coming from enemy positions to the south. The Enemy troops would defiantly stand in the open, firing their AK-47s as the jets came in for their bomb run. The jet flashed over the NVA position, dropping a canister of napalm on the unsuspecting enemy. Sheehy was startled to see the tree line explode into a ball of fire. He could feel the heat from the blaze and hear the screams from the enemy soldiers as they staggered around in flames. The paddy was lit for some time due to the thick vegetation.

Barnes was awakened by the heat, noticing the tree line on fire. A short time later, he heard the sound of a propeller driven aircraft. It appeared to be circling the area where the Jets had dropped the napalm. Suddenly, a cone of red fire streamed from the side of the circling plane, reaching all the way to the ground. The light beam was followed by an ear-piercing sound, similar to a foghorn. He had seen its destruction before during night fire fights. The sound was indescribable; a deep, guttural roar that anyone who has ever heard it and lived through it, will always remember. Each gatling gun firing 100 rounds per second. Puff the Magic Dragon had lit up the sky with its fiery, red breath.

When the drone from the huge engines faded into the distance, there was a deathly silence that lingered over the battlefield. Nothing moved in the eerie glare of the flare, as it floated slowly to Earth.

Over the period of a couple hours, Sheehy moved himself across the paddy. Crossing the paddy dikes was the most difficult part of his slow journey. In the darkness, he would shove his body into a seated position against a dike, slide up onto the dike, then pull his legs onto the dike, then use his momentum to roll off onto the other side.

Upon reaching one of the dikes, he realized he had pushed himself next to the booted foot of a dead Marine. His body lay face up on the other side. In the light of the next flare, he identified the body as that of Sergeant Ackley. He had crawled clear across the paddy to where it all began for him. Lying next to his Sergeant, he recalled that he carried a pistol. Sheehy felt along the Sergeant's body until he came to the holster attached to his web belt. The holster still contained the 45-pistol. Removing the pistol with his good hand, he now had a weapon. He wouldn't know if a round was chambered until the time came when he actually needed to use it.

Sheehy eventually passed out from exhaustion and would not wake up until the sky turned gray in the east.

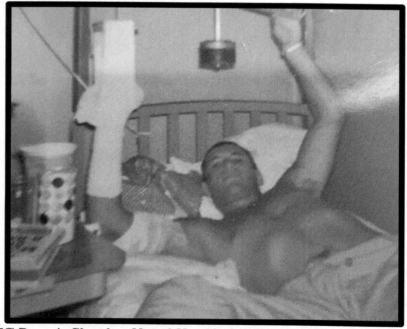

PFC Dennis Sheehy, Naval Hospital in Bremerton, Washington

As Lance Corporal Gobrecht slowly moved from one paddy dike to the next, he would occasionally hear enemy voices, fueling him forward; hobbling on his left leg while stabbing pain radiated throughout his body. When flares illuminated the battlefield, the eeriness of the dead surrounding him was haunting. The light danced across their contorted faces, creating the illusion of life. Finally, he heard other Marines as they tried to get back to Hills A and B. They were moving wounded towards the evacuation area. He begged them for water, but after they inspected the injuries to his stomach, they denied his request for fear that shrapnel may have torn his intestines. Sometime around 0230 hours, he was evacuated with five other wounded Marines.

First Lieutenant John Updyke was the forward air controller for Lieutenant Colonel Hilgartner's First Battalion. Lt. Updyke provided fire support from the start of the engagement until the enemy began their withdrawal on June 3, somewhere around 0330 hours. He managed close air support, better known as "Spooky" fire or "Puff the Magic Dragon" and close artillery support, continuously for five to six hours. Much of this time was spent exposing himself to the enemy in an effort to observe and provide accurate fire on their positions.

2400 HOURS:

Sometime after midnight, Corporal Barnes continued his movement in the paddy towards Hill A. The progress was slow as he dragged his shattered arms through the rice paddy. His left arm with the severed artery began to bleed again. Using his teeth and right elbow, he was able to tighten the tourniquet and lessen the blood loss.

A heavy mist and fog had settled over the battlefield during the night. Lieutenant Colonel Hilgartner received a radio call from his Delta Company Commander, Mack McInturff. The NVA had litter bearers out in the paddy collecting their dead and wounded. They used two poles with material in between, similar to the ones used by the Native American Indians to transport their sick and injured across the prairies of America. They were seen just to the right flank of Fox Company's dead and wounded, laying in the rice paddy. He feared they were looking for wounded Marines, either Captain Graham's or Delta's. Mack requested permission to fire on them. Lieutenant Colonel Hilgartner saw it as an opportunity to retrieve our own dead and wounded.

"Mack, you will only fire if the enemy starts shooting at our people. Is that clear?"

McInturff contacted Lieutenant Bill Link, his Third Platoon Commander, to organize a search party and go into the rice paddies to look for the wounded and dead. Updyke suspended the battlefield illumination to prevent the enemy from firing on the search party.

Corporal Barnes spotted two Marines standing by a large tree somewhere in the area of Hills one and two. The two Marines must have seen Barnes' movement in the rice paddy. They both stood by the tree waving for him to come to their location. At first, he wondered why they wouldn't just come and help him, but then it dawned on him, no Marine wanted to go into the killing fields in the darkness of the night.

Barnes, for the first time since he had entered the rice paddy hours before, decided to get up and attempt to make his way to the Marines. He moved as quickly as possible, waiting for a sniper's bullet to put an end to his misery, but a bullet never came. He made it within a few feet of the tree before falling to the ground. He crawled the rest of the way and leaned against its trunk. Looking up at the two Delta Company Marines, he could see the Sergeant insignias on the collars of one of them, "Sergeant, let Command know, there is no more Fox, Second Platoon, they're all dead, including Captain Graham."

The two Marines assisted Barnes in getting to the evacuation area that had been cleared from the heavy, jungle foliage. The clearing was packed with wounded Marines everywhere. The Battalion Surgeon was moving from one wounded Marine to the other. As he checked the wounds on Barnes' body, he looked up at the Surgeon, "Doc, could you check the dressing on my left arm and don't let them take off my arm." The dressing had been bound tightly for over eight hours and Barnes was worried about nerve paralysis and limb ischemia, resulting in amputation.

Within the next hour, he heard a UH-34 circling above the medevac zone. Feeling the wind from the blades, he knew the pilot was attempting to land. No landing lights were being used because of the enemy being in such close proximity. Barnes could see the tight medevac area, no more than 10' x 10' and he wondered how the pilot was going to land.

As the helicopter lowered, one of the landing skids came down no more than a foot from his head. The door gunner jumped out hollering, "Give me six badly wounded! Give me six wounded, fast!" Barnes watched and counted as each Marine was thrown through the doorway of the Huey.

At the count of five, the door gunner hollered again, "One more! Quickly!" pointing to Barnes. Two Marines picked him up and threw him through the doorway. He landed on top of the other five Marines.

The chopper lifted off the ground with the Marines stacked on top of one another. They hollered and shouted, "Get off of me! Get off of me!" Crawling over bodies, Barnes found a small corner on the floor of the Huey.

The moment had come that Barnes thought he would never see. He was on his way off the battlefield of the deadliest fight that Second Platoon would ever see during the Vietnam War.

> The 2nd Battalion, 5th Marines' After-Action Report for Operation UNION II contains the following entry:
>
> (6) 021200H Company F advanced to search the area vicinity coordinates (BT 107314) at approximately 021205H, and while moving through the area encountered scattered resistance resulting in 5 NVA KIA confirmed. The company continued down into the flat paddy land at vicinity coordinates (BT 107314) when a Kit Carson scout started shooting at flat mats of hay laying in the paddy. The NVA had concealed themselves under the hay mats and 31 NVA KIA confirmed were counted as Company F advanced. At approximately 021420H, heavy enemy mortar, rocket, small arms and automatic weapons fire were received from vicinity coordinates (BT 094314) from an estimated 300-500 enemy in a heavily fortified trench position. The enemy fire stopped Company F, which consolidated their position and brought heavy fire on the enemy position. At approximately 021520H the reserve platoon was maneuvered to secure the high ground. The platoon assaulted the enemy position and there were 35 NVA KIA confirmed. At approximately 021730H the Company F commander led an assault on the enemy defensive command bunker, personally killing 15 NVA before he was killed trying to secure a machine gun bunker. The acting company commander consolidated into nigh positions vicinity coordinates (BT 100315) a approximately 021920H and called in artillery and airstrikes throughout the night. Results of the engagement: 170 KIA confirmed, 310 NVA KIA probable, 32 USMC KIA, 39 USMC WIA.

8.3 *The Walking Dead*

I do not fear death for it will be the opportunity to reunite with brothers lost on the Field of Valor. I know that for the rest of my life when for no reason, I seem to go silent. Even when I'm right next to you, remember two words and you will know where I am.

— *"The Battlefield"*

Shortly before sunrise, while the skies were still dark, Staff Sergeant Marengo had just finished checking the positions and condition of his men. Returning to the CP area, Tony noticed Gunnery Sergeant Green and First sergeant Lee huddled together away from the other Marines. Walking over to their location, he could hear them whispering words of how this battle reminded them of being back in Korea. Both Marines had fought on the Korean battlefields. He could hear them saying how the enemy yesterday fought with the intensity of the Chinese. They never thought they would be in a war or in a battle again like the one they had experienced on those battlefields in Korea.

When Marengo got closer, he could see them wiping their eyes. He understood their pain from the night before and decided not to press the subject.

The few remaining Marines of Fox Company would spend the rest of the night sitting in their defensive positions with M-16 rifles that didn't work and a helmet full of hand grenades, waiting for an enemy counterattack that would never come.

By daylight, the enemy had pulled off the battlefield. Now came the daunting task of removing the dead Marines and equipment.

A handful of survivors from Fox Company along with troopers from Echo Company, a sister company to Fox, moved out into the rice paddy.

When additional helicopters landed to evacuate the last of the wounded and load the dead, the surviving Marines were surprised by a bunch of national reporters, taking up much needed chopper space. The last thing the Marines wanted or needed was "press" questioning them about the events that had occurred the previous night and early morning. The troops were thirsty, tired, hungry and really pissed off. Corporal Pat Halley, a Rocketman from Third Platoon, explained it like this:

"When dawn finally came, we discovered that the surviving NVA had departed the rice paddy. The paddy now lay in deathly, ominous, unforgiving silence. No amnesty here, no congressman's sons either! Only blood, guts and body bags. What a gut wrenching, unforgettable experience. Regardless of our exhaustion, no sleep and more importantly, our overwhelming reluctance to face and identify our dead, we, the surviving Marines of Foxtrot, had to do what had to be done and we did it tearfully. I must admit, in war zones it does not take long to get very close to your fellow Marines."

Ken Kreader, one of the surviving Marines tasked with loading the dead onto helicopters, revealed that the stench "is a smell that just does not come off for some time."

The formidable tree line, part of Objective Foxtrot, where Corporal Barnes lay during the night and morning of June 3, was the hardest for the recovery teams to deal with. It was where the bodies of Captain Graham and Lieutenant Kelsey lay. Many of the bodies along that tree line could only be identified through forensics. It was where most of the heavy bombing and napalm was dropped; the smoldering trees and shredded vegetation told part of the tale.

Staff Sergeant Tony Marengo later said, "I don't know how anyone survived in and around that tree line."

The troops spread out throughout the 1,000 m rice paddy, silently placing their former brothers or whatever parts they could find, into body bags and searching for weapons and equipment. PFC Mike Hernandez moved into the rice paddy to assist in the removal of the dead Marines. The first Marine he came to was his Platoon Sergeant Gerald Ackley. He still had his shotgun lying next to him. Once he reached the tree line, he saw Monfils, Byrd, Driscoll and others. He found Captain Graham face-down.

Someone hollered, "Don't move him! They might have him booby trapped." Ignoring the warning, Mike Hernandez and another Marine turned him over. They gathered the Marines and waited for a chopper to come and pick them up. Over to their right, some Marine Officers were being interviewed by the media. They walked over to the machine gun emplacement that had the Marines pinned down the day before. The gun emplacement that had killed so many Marines. Enemy bodies still lay in and around the trench line. The same gun emplacement Corporal Barnes, along with Gobrecht and O'Brien, had assaulted. It was a seven-foot-deep hole with a tunnel leading all the way back to the village behind the tree line. At the top, was a sitting position to fire the machine gun. The gunner would fire the weapon and was able to drop down into the tunnel during an airstrike.

It took all day to clear the battlefield. The airstrikes had torn many of the bodies apart and they were strewn in every direction. The survivors were emotionally and psychologically exhausted. It was one of the worst days of their lives.

Colonel Houghton, who had asked for 2/5's most aggressive Company, flew in on the third to visit Fox Company's few survivors. Most had been wounded but not evacuated. He addressed the survivors who were left, "Marines, I put Fox into the center of the breach and your company was the lynchpin in defeating an enemy regiment. I had always heard of your fighting ability…your braveness. Today you have exceeded your reputation. You men exemplify the heroic character of the Fifth Marine Regiment and the United States Marine Corps. With you, I mourn your losses. We can never bring them back. They were brave Marines who did not die in vain. Men of Foxtrot, I salute you and your magnificent fighting company." The Colonel gave a hand salute while turning to all Marines and Corpsmen to ensure they had been recognized.

The enemy Commander, Colonel Giap Van Cuong of the Second Division, Third Regiment of the North Vietnamese Army, must be given credit. He had his troops well positioned to defend against the Marines' assault. He used his time well when recovering his wounded, to cover his withdrawal of the main force of his troops, to fight another day. He must've known that because of our large number of casualties and the many enemy bodies he left on the battlefield, we would not pursue him until all our dead and wounded had been recovered and we had counted his KIA's. Whether or not he knew this was First Marine Division's policy, his strategy worked well. We would count his dead and satisfy MACV Headquarters, giving them their body count in order to bolster their, "light at the end of the tunnel."

Total marine losses on Union II from May 26 to June 2 was 110 men killed and 241 wounded. It was the sixth deadliest battle of the Vietnam War. During the month-long battle for the Hue City from February 2 to March 2, 1968, which was the fifth deadliest battle, there were a total of 119 men killed. In the siege of Khe Sanh from January 20, 1968 to April 14, 1968, the second deadliest battle, a total of 205 men were killed in action. On June 2, 1967, Fox 2/5 proportionately lost more of their Marines than any other American Infantry Company during the entire Vietnam War. They would receive the Presidential Unit Citation.

The Marines counted 476 dead North Vietnamese soldiers in and around the contested rice paddy and its formidable hedgerow complex. A total of over 700 dead NVA throughout the entire battlefield. The Marines themselves suffered 71 killed and 139 wounded in the fight.

A large majority of the Marines who died were not old enough to buy a beer back in the States. Of the 32 Marines killed in Fox Company, 23 of them or 72%, were 20 years old or younger.

Over the next two days, the Marines of Fox Company finished clearing equipment from the battlefield. Helicopters brought the equipment to An Hoa. Fox Company worked in parties, hauling the packs, helmets and other field equipment from the airstrip to the Company Headquarters.

After the battlefield was cleared of all the dead Marines and equipment on June 4, at 1400 hours, helicopters landed to take what few survivors were left of Fox Company back to the base camp at An Hoa. The Marines' eyes and minds remained locked on the battlefield as the choppers lifted off from the rice paddies of Union II.

1400 HOURS:

June 4, No one anticipated the reception as they landed at the airstrip in An Hoa. Over 100 Marines and Corpsmen from Echo Company, Hotel Company and their supporting elements of the Second Battalion, gathered around the landing choppers. Silence greeted them. The salute showed the respect and sincere admiration felt for their fellow Marines as the men of An Hoa welcomed the surviving heroes home.

PFC Terry Klein

When Terry Klein got off the returning chopper in An Hoa from Union II, he was dirty, tired, unshaven and wearing the same jungle utilities he had worn for the past week. He walked back to the hooch where his Third Platoon was assigned.

The hooches at An Hoa, where the Marines of Fox Company stayed when not in the jungle on operations or patrols, were set alongside 105 and 155 howitzer artillery installations for the base camp.

A hooch was made of plywood and two by fours, screened in with a metal roof. Setting right next to the artillery, all night long, you could hear the artillery radios blaring and rounds being fired from the guns. The plywood building would shake every time a gun would fire. It was so bad you couldn't hang anything up. Things would even vibrate at night, falling onto the floor or onto your sleeping rack.

Returning to the hooch Terry could not find any of his gear, it was not around his rack area. He immediately went to the supply Sergeant to find out where it had gone.

"My name is Terry Klein. What the hell happened to all my gear in my hooch?"

"Oh, you're Terry Klein. Your gear is over there in that hooch," replied the Sergeant as he pointed to an area.

"Why in the hell is it over there Sergeant?"

"It's next to Gary Kline's gear. We didn't know which Klein died, one or both," the Sergeant answered candidly.

Gary Kline died on June 2, fighting with the Marines in Second Platoon. Terry Klein of Third Platoon survived to return to base camp and fight another day.

Lance Corporal Perry Jones was a good friend of both Barnes and Gobrecht. Perry was one of Barnes' squad leaders in the Third Platoon. As soon as he returned to An Hoa, he wanted to let his two friends know how he had survived the battle.

Returning to his platoon hut he immediately sat down to write a letter to John Gobrecht:

Dear John,   June 4, 1967

Well, here I am alive and in pretty good health, but I wish I could be with you! After the battle, I tried to find you, but they told me that the whole second squad of guns had been wiped out and I'll tell you now, I felt like crying!! I guess you're home by now or at least in good care by a nice-looking nurse and I sure hope you feel at least better.

I lost two men, but the rest will be alright and that's all I could ask for, right? O'Brien was killed and Barnes was wounded pretty bad and the rest were wounded, but we had 34 killed and I was sick. If I ever have to pick up another dead person, I'll go crazy as a bat and that's no lie! Boy was I ever glad to hear you made it and I'm glad to know you're going back to the states. I only wish I could be there with you.

I'm supposed to be section leader now, but all we got left are eight men and three machine guns. Well enough of this place, I've got your records and record player and if I get enough money, I'll send them to you as soon as possible, all right?

I guess I'll say good-bye, take care of yourself and write me soon from life alright? May God bless and keep you safe and I hope to see you soon.

A friend always,
Perry

218

Later that evening, after Terry was able to shower and put on a new pair of jungle fatigues, he was told by Staff Sergeant Marengo to go to the CP and get the mail. Terry walked into the command hooch and saw First Sergeant Lee sitting at his desk. Lee was writing something down on a piece of paper. The First Sergeant looked up with tears dripping onto the paper, visibly upset.

Terry turned around to leave the Sergeant in peace, when he heard, "Marine get your ass back in here! Writing these letters home to dead Marines' families is something I never wanted to do while in this command."

"Sir, I was told to come here and get the mail for the Third Platoon."

"The bag's over there in the corner and on your way out there's eight guys outside, replacements straight from the states, take them back with you to the Third Platoon."

Walking out of the command hooch he saw the Marines going through a pile of gear. They had been told to get a flak jacket and magazines from the pile. He could see them going through the pile of magazines, trying to find ones that weren't covered in blood stains. He stood there for a few minutes watching them. He saw every Marine picking up four magazines for their M-16 rifle.

Realizing they were only taking four, because that's what they were issued in infantry training, he promptly corrected them, "You guys need to grab at least eight mags, when you get out in the bush, you're going to need every one of them and wish you had more."

He watched as the Marines grabbed 4 more magazines. Terry knew these poor guys were coming in immediately after a major battle as replacements for a lot of dead

Marines. He wondered what they were thinking as he walked them back to the Third Platoon.

First Sergeant Lee and Gunnery Sergeant Green were part of the rebuilding process. Lance Corporal Mackinnon became the battalion radio operator, Lee had Dave Anderson promoted to Lance Corporal and assigned him to replace Mackinnon as a company radio operator. When PFC Mike Hernandez returned to An Hoa, he was assigned to Corporal Eddie Roberts' squad in Second Platoon. Roberts had not participated in Union II. Roberts was recovering from an earlier punji stick injury where he lost his entire squad on Union II and was mourning the loss of all his friends.

As other replacements arrived to rebuild Fox Company, Mike was reminded of being back in the staging battalion at Camp Pendleton in January of 1967. A veteran Marine had quipped, "I've been to Vietnam, not all of you will make it back."

LaBarbera, the prior company clerk who survived being bombed and shot at, was glad to be back in the rear and less anxious to go on the next operation if they were all going to be like Union II. He did provide good advice to the replacements who had to pass through him before being assigned to a platoon.

Union II had only added to the reputation that Fox Company upheld as they started to become known as "Fatal Fox."

This is how Lance Corporal Brent "Mac" Mackinnon describes the situation as he got off the helicopter at An Hoa Base on June 4, 1967.

Talking With the Dead

An Hoa Base:

I am a hollow statue wearing a skin of ragged uniform, gear, weapons and dirt; I have no body. Floating in a bad dream, we few survivors climb down off the helicopters. Zombies in filthy fatigues, some partially clothed some in bandages, others dazed and supported by companions.

Impotent and armed only with a pencil, our Fox Company admin clerk stands, counting bodies as we stagger towards the double line of huts and hooches.
His name? My mind is numb. He recognizes me.

"Mac!"

I keep moving, going...somewhere.
His lips move again.

"Johnson?"

I shake my head.

"Driscoll? The Mortar Squad?"

A voice moves through me, whispers, "No."

I keep moving. Our hooch looks 1000 m away and in the same moment, I feel wooden steps under my feet. The screen door squeaks, as always, as though nothing has happened. Inside the silent space, cots and footlockers stand squared away, waiting for their Marines.

Lying on his stolen bookshelf are Joe's phonograph and pirated record albums from R & R in Bangkok. New letters from Driscoll's mom scatter across his rack. Sarges collection of popular mechanics remains stacked under his cot. Next to Mike's pillow, a pencil pokes out, saving a place in his poetry notebook. Our hooch stands ready for their return. Faithful and intimate possessions wait to be brought to life again by human touch. Now these things too are dead, tombstones in a graveyard full of ghosts. Rows of cots, like empty coffins, await bodies they once comforted. Everyone dead. Everyone, but me.

Someone moves off to the left. Who violates this holy ground? With a hand on my pistol and the evil eye, I turn and stare down the stranger. An old man, filthy, bearded, with dead eyes stares back.

I confront him. "What the fuck are you look—"

His mouth is open. He moves as I move. I am yelling, challenging a mirror. A stranger. What happened to me? The person I remember just a few days ago is no more. The old man stares back and I see in his eyes a part of me, lying out in that rice paddy in a body bag.

I sit down on the end of my cot. I want to cry; need to cry. But there are no tears in this gray shadow land I have entered into. But I know now, I will survive. They can't kill a ghost.

-Brent "Mac" Mackinnon

8.4 *The Long Road Home*

"I came home and tried to not let the scars affect me, but the war had changed me. I had killed men and seen men killed. I had lived when others more deserving of life had perished. I'm a different person now."
  -Rick Barnes

Corporal Barnes' experience in war had left a profound and strangely compelling effect on him. He had seen the horrors of combat on the battlefield and it had revealed the power of brotherhood; a selfless sense of purpose. He had joined the military at the age of 17 and went to war. Most of the Marines serving with him were no more than 18 or 19 years old. Rick had never been away from home and had little experience in the world, let alone in a war with death and killing. For him, combat was a complex mix of emotions. It was the worst thing in the world, inflicting both physical and emotional injuries, yet it was insanely exciting.

The self-sacrifice among his fellow Marines was evident in the bond they had formed. Rick's life had never mattered more than it did when he was in combat; when he had a sense of meaning and purpose that was derived from protecting and being protected. It was a shared commitment to safeguard one another's lives that was non-negotiable and had only deepened with time. The experiences and terror of combat had imprinted on Rick in a way that the word "brother" could only partly capture.

Sometimes killing would seem like an easy act, but it had consequences. You were confronted with this sense of euphoria from being the survivor; this primal feeling of being the victorious predator that conquered its prey. But there was also this contentious concept of taking a life and the emotions that wash over you from such a final act. When you tried to make sense of the two, the troubling question

224

became, "I just killed and I am happy about it, does that mean I like killing?"

In tourniquet blood loss injuries, the key to survival is rapid blood loss replacement. The time it took to get from the battlefield to the field hospital, was crucial. It had been well over eight hours since Corporal Barnes had incurred his most critical wound, a severed artery. Ideal survival rate was the first hour. It was called, "The Golden Hour" by the military medical staff. His other obstacle was the fact that he had laid in a muddy, rice paddy for eight hours, making his wounds prone to infection.

Vietnam was the first major conflict to use helicopters to get injured soldiers out of combat zones so they could be transferred as quickly as possible to the military hospitals. A soldier could be injured one hour and be in surgery the next.

The job of the Second Surgical Combat Hospital in Chu Lai was to stabilize the injured before sending them to more remote hospitals. In many cases, back into battle.

When the helicopter arrived at Chu Lai from the battlefield, Corporal Barnes was taken into a steel quonset hut with screened windows, no air-conditioning and no running water. His wounds were stabilized and temporary arm casts were placed on both arms. A few hours later, Rick found himself in a temporary holding hallway with other injured soldiers.

One of the injured soldiers to his right was a helicopter Flight Captain. Barnes asked the Captain, "How did you end up here?"

"I was one of the pilots getting wounded out of Union II last night. We came under heavy fire and I was shot through the windshield of the chopper."

The soldier to his left was a South Korean Marine. After the Marines fought to give South Korea freedom from the Chinese, the Korean War ended. They named their Army after the United States Marines and were now fighting alongside the Marines in Vietnam. Looking at Barnes, the soldier kept pointing at his bare chest and with a big smile on his face, he kept saying, "Zipper, zipper." The Korean Marine had been cut open from his neck all the way to his belly button, with large stitches running the whole length. Unable to speak Korean, I was never able to get the rest of the story.

On June 3, 1967, sometime during the night, Rick was placed on a medevac aircraft and transported to the Clark Air Force Base in the Philippines. He was quickly taken into the hospital and placed in a hospital ward. Rick didn't remember much about the medevac or being placed in the hospital ward. The exhaustion from battle had finally taken its toll.

The next few days Rick spent in surgery and having his wounds cleaned. Casts weren't put back on his arms because they needed to monitor the wound sites in order to ensure no infection was present. Within a few days, their suspicions were confirmed, infection had set in.

The next few weeks, Rick endured the most pain he had ever experienced in his lifetime. During the daily scrubbing and cleaning of the open wounds, the military orderlies spared no mercy. Finally, on June 7, 1967, Rick was able to physically and mentally, write his first letter.

My Darling Wife,   June 7, 1967

Honey, I am writing this letter. I hope you can read it.

I am in the Philippines at a Naval Hospital. Tomorrow I leave for Washington DC. From there I hope to go to the Great Lakes Naval Hospital. You will be able to come and see me all the time until I'm OK again. In less than two months I'll be all well again. Maybe it will take a little longer for my left arm. We will be able to start our life together a lot sooner than we thought. I'm really anxious to see you.

You're probably wondering just how bad I'm hurt. Well, my left arm is broken just below the wrist. I have about a 4-inch cut along my right forearm which is also broken below the elbow. My next to the last knuckle on my right hand is broken and I have another small cut on the backside of the upper part of my right arm. I have four cuts in different parts of my right leg. I can walk and do most things myself. If I can't do it myself, I find a way.

Honey, I am so glad to be getting out of Vietnam for good. I really left no friends in Vietnam, because they're all dead. Only five of us made it out alive that night from the platoon I was with. We tried to hold the VC off but that evening they overran us. That night somehow I managed to make it back to friendly lines. Don't ask me how I did it cause it was a work of God. The guys that couldn't crawl away were killed by the VC that night.

FRONTLINE BROTHERS

You probably heard about the 73 Marines killed June 2. Well quite a few of those dead were my platoon and the command group which was attached. The rest were killed in the fighting which took place around us by Marines trying to break through to help us but help never came. Second Platoon Foxtrot died that night. I died with them Suzanne. Part of me and all my memories. I made it through that day until about 5 o'clock. Finally, the VC decided to make their final push to overrun us. They started dropping 82 mortars and RPG's in on us. One landed about 8 yards from me at the most. Shrapnel hit me all over. I had already been wounded a couple times earlier in the battle.

I wanted you to know what happened, I'll probably never talk about it again. I want to try and forget it all. Although I know I never will. If they take me to Great Lakes, I'll get a hold of you and let you know.

Tell our moms and dads that I'm sorry I can't write but I should get to see them all soon. Honey, I love you so very much. I'll be able to tell you real soon.

Honey I've seen death and I know what real life is. I can't wait to live that real life with you. Honey, we've got so much living ahead of us. I'll be closing for now. Be good baby, I love you.

Your loving husband,
Rick

The next morning a Red Cross worker came walking into Rick's room, white uniform and all.

"Are you Corporal Barnes?"

"Yes ma'am, I am."

"I have a message for you, you're going to be a father."

Not totally surprised, he thanked her as she walked away. After all, two months ago while on R & R in Hawaii, he had hardly left the hotel room...

Susann had contacted the local National Red Cross in the states and asked to get the message to me. It wasn't for another week until Rick was notified that he'd be catching a medevac flight back to the Great Lakes Naval Hospital the following day. That evening, arm casts were again, placed on both broken arms for the transport home.

Early the next morning, Rick was taken by military ambulance onto the tarmac at the military airbase. As the rear doors opened, he was placed on a forklift platform and raised to the level of the rear exit, then carried by stretcher onto the aircraft where the stretcher was attached to the side of the fuselage. The stretchers were placed two high, getting the bottom row afforded Rick the window seat; he was one of the lucky ones.

Another section of the aircraft contained patients who had less serious injuries. They were able to walk from the ambulance to the plane; boarding and taking their seats as if they were passengers on a commercial flight.

The flying ambulance was an Air Force plane flown by a Navy crew and flight attendants.

The aircraft spat puffs of white smoke as her four engines roared to life with her destination being the United States. Soon the plane was racing over the concrete runway, airborne, as the twin-peaked Mount Arayat faded into the distance.

A female Air Force Captain, Anna Lee, was the head flight nurse in charge. She carried a clipboard with several sheets of paper containing the names of all the men on board along with their injuries. As she walked down the center of the aircraft, she asked each soldier their name and how they felt. She had the scent of a Georgia peach blossom straight from the orchard. Her sweet accent simply added to her southern charm.

The crew was well on its way to Anchorage Alaska for refueling. Having a window view of the sky above the clouds, watching them float by allowed Rick's mind to wander. He was now separated from his Foxtrot Company brothers and surrounded by soldiers he didn't know. They were all survivors of the same war, but had endured many different battles. As he scanned the rows of soldiers, some with bandages wrapped around their heads, some with a leg missing or an arm gone, some with casts like himself, he wondered what disability would he suffer? What wounds was he taking home with him?

Little did he realize at the time, but his biggest battle yet would be with himself. The war was only beginning. For years, Rick would stuff Vietnam in a box and put it away, until one day, when he was no longer able to keep the lid closed...

As the aircraft was making its final run for landing, he could see American soil for the first time in months. In a very short time, he had developed a bit of an attitude, feeling sorry for himself. When the plane touched down, he looked out the window, thinking how America owed him something.

That would be short-lived because he was about to arrive at the Great Lakes Naval Hospital. And his first-hand account of his experiences there, would forever change his outlook on life.

We were only in Anchorage long enough for refueling and were back in the air in no time. Our next stop was the Great Lakes and we didn't get in until the middle of the night. Upon landing at O'Hare Airport in Chicago, I soon arrived at the entrance to a hospital ward called 3-South.

In the middle of the night, at 2:00 AM, I was wheeled, on a gurney, into the darkened ward. It had been a long flight and I immediately fell asleep after being placed in my hospital bed.

The next morning, I awoke and looked at the bed to my left. It was a Marine staring at nothing, towards the windows to his front. He had been a Tank Commander and his tank had run over a booby-trapped 250-pound bomb in Vietnam. The blast had blown him out of the top turret, catching both legs on the edge of the turret; they were severed just above the knee. Looking towards the bed to my right was a Marine by the last name of White. He had detonated a bomb which took off both legs, both arms and one eye.

Little did I know, but last night I was placed in the Great Lakes Naval Hospital "Amputee-Infection Ward."

Laying in my hospital bed, I looked down at my feet and wiggled my toes. With my fingers sticking out the ends of two arm casts, I wiggled my fingers.

In my head I said to myself, *this country does not owe me anything, they owe it to the Marine to my left and the one to my right*. From that day on, I would never feel sorry for myself again.

I spent three months at the Great Lakes Naval Hospital being treated for my wounds and convalescing. Susann along with my mother, father and brothers were finally able to come visit. Susann drove at least once a week from Northwest Indiana to see me. Just like the rest of the soldiers on 3-South, I tried to make the best of it. Pranks were often played on each other and sometimes even the staff were the brunt of some laughs.

The elevators were located just outside the double doors to the ward. One of the elevators led down to the basement where the hospital morgue was located. When a patient died of complications from their injuries, they would be taken to the basement. A gurney always set outside the elevator door with a sheet nicely folded on one end, awaiting the next body needing to be taken down. After the first couple weeks, I was one of the few on the ward that was mobile and could get out of bed. Which meant, I was the first to volunteer for the fun.

The plan was to go to the elevator door, get on the gurney, cover up with the sheet and wait to be taken to the morgue. It didn't take long for one of the orderlies to see the sheet-covered body waiting to be taken down, so into the elevator I went. The Marines on the ward did their best to control their laughter and not give away the plan. As the elevator descended and came to a stop, I could feel the cold air rush in as the door opened; a chill that went straight to my core. I had arrived. I listened intently as I heard the freezer door open. For fear I would actually be placed in the freezer alive, I decided to get on with the prank and jumped up into a seated position. The orderly about damn near had a heart attack and fell back from the gurney; a scared-shitless look covering his face. As the two of us went back up in the elevator, the orderly was calling Rick every name in the book. As they entered the double doors of 3-South, applause and laughter rang out across the ward.

A few weeks after that, an announcement was made that Hugh Hefner would be sending over three playboy bunnies to entertain us. The Chicago playboy mansion was having a meet and great for the Marines of 3-South.

For most of us, it had been months since we had seen a girl, let alone a bunny, and likely even longer since we had been with one.

Everything went as expected. Excitement was in the air and anyone who desired a signed autographed picture of a bunny of their choice, was given one. It seemed like for the remainder of the day, the bunnies were all us Marines could talk about until we fell asleep.

Word was passed through the ward the next morning that one of the Marines had died during the night. When I got up that morning to walk around, I passed the empty bed of the Marine. On his nightstand was still the signed autograph of one of the Playboy bunnies.

While in the ward, I received a letter from Lance Corporal "Mac" McAnaly, my good friend who was also in the Union II battle. He was the second man wounded by the same grenade that struck me, before we moved down into the rice paddy for the final assault. Mac was able to get on the first medevac chopper that was called in. He was stitched up and sent right back to the Second Platoon within a month.

Dear Barney,   Monday, July 17, 1967

Well, Barney things aren't so good we got hit harder than hell up at the coal mines on the 4th of July. Right on top of the hill where 4.2 mortars stay 1st Platoon had the top again this time.

There were approximately 500 VC. 150 of them made it to the top.

They had AK-47 automatic rifles, submachine guns, satchel charges, M-26's and gook grenades. There were nine people killed from the 1st platoon. Everybody else in 1st Platoon was wounded. The 1st platoon is gone now and they're building it back up. Some of the guys in 1st who were killed or Joe Hicks, Tony Alonso, he's the guy who always wore that silk camouflage scarf around his neck. Ball, Currey and Newland. Newland is the guy who was always on missed duty. He was in 1st Plt. Guns.

The same night they dropped over 80 mortar rounds on An Hoa plus 140 mm rockets. Three were killed and about 10 or 15 wounded. That same night Echo Company was mortared in Antenna Valley. They had one wounded. Now here comes the hard part. O'Brien is dead and you know about everybody else. I think only six people from 2nd platoon. Pagan, Legere, Brown, Herrell, Dickerson and Hernandez. Oh yes and Doc Schmit. A couple of the guys cracked and had to be sent to Japan. That day really fucked up some of the guys. Mackinnon and Little both made it from the CP group, as did Gy/Sgt Greene.

Sorry to have to write to you and tell you all this bad news. You know as well as I do not too much good news comes out of a place like this.

I'll be getting out of here real soon now. My brother is in 7th comm. section in Da Nang. He told me to get my young ass back to the rock. I'm going to do just that.

Well Barn, if there's anything you want to know that I left out just drop me a line. Drop me a line anyway.

Your buddy
Mac - L/Cpl Type

PS. I'll be a father in 2 weeks. How's that for helping the population explosion?

A couple of weeks prior to being released from Great Lakes Naval Hospital, Corporal Barnes was notified that he was to receive the Silver Star for his actions on June 2nd. The Commandant of the Marine Corps would be coming to Great Lakes Naval Hospital to make the presentation.

CPL Rick Barnes receiving the Silver Star at Great Lakes Naval Hospital

Shortly after the presentation, Corporal Barnes was promoted to Sergeant and received orders to report to the 27th Marines in Camp Pendleton California.

Susann arrived at Camp Pendleton with Rick and they moved into an apartment off base in San Clemente. Shortly after arriving, Sergeant Barnes was told that another surgery was needed on his left arm. It took place at the Camp Pendleton base hospital. During recovery, Barnes was given the temporary duty as Supply Sergeant.

RICK BARNES

By the latter part of 1967 he could gradually see the Second and Third Battalions of the 27th Marines being brought up to full strength.

By December 1967, word was being circulated around the Regiment that the 28th Marines were going to Vietnam. Sergeant Barnes was advised by his Company Commander that he would be going to Vietnam with the unit as well. Realizing that his wife Susann was due with their baby the first week of January and was unable to fly, he immediately submitted a request for one week leave to drive his wife back to her family in northwest Indiana. He let the Captain know that he would rejoin the company no matter what phase of deployment they were in. The request was denied.

Sergeant Barnes went to the Company Command hut to speak to the company clerk.

"Corporal, any word on when you think we are going to ship out?"

"Could be any day Barnes."

"Damn, I've got to get my wife home she's due any day."

"You know Barnes, when you first joined the company, I was looking at your service record, you've got two Purple Hearts. You know you can opt out with two hearts."

"Great, let the Captain know I am opting out."

On January 10, 1968, Tracie Marie Barnes was born at the Camp Pendleton base hospital in the state of California. By January 1968, in response to the Tet Offensive in Vietnam, President Johnson formerly authorized an increase in troop strength.

On February 12, 1968, in response to the increase, the 27th Marines were headed to Vietnam. 3300 Marines of the Second and Third Battalions were flown by the military airlift command planes to Da Nang, Vietnam. Sergeant Barnes would not be on that flight. The First Battalion stationed in Hawaii would arrive in Da Nang by troop transport ships. With the 27th Marines departure, Barnes was transferred to India Company, Third Battalion, 28th Marines, Fifth Marine Division. The battalion was being maintained as a reaction force and training unit for personnel bound for Vietnam. Sergeant Barnes would assume training duties for new replacements and would receive a Meritorious Mast from the Regimental Commander.

Staff Sergeant Barnes received an honorable discharge from the Marine Corps on April 1, 1969.

Barnes had considered a career in the Marine Corps, but realized that an old saying in the Corps was holding true: *During wartime, if the Marine Corps wanted you to have a wife, they would have issued you one.*

Rick returned to northwest Indiana where he pursued a career in law-enforcement, going on to become a successful home builder. His second daughter, Tonya Lynn Barnes, was born on January 12, 1971.

THE BATTLE NEVER ENDS

People would ask, "Why did you go to Vietnam? Do you love war? Do you like killing?"

9.1 *The War Inside My Head*

When I got home, that's what people would ask. There wasn't much I could say in response; they wouldn't have understood. It's not possible for people to understand the hell we experienced unless they have experienced war themselves. It was about the Marine next to you and that's it. That's all it was. If you focused on anything else beyond that, you wouldn't have made it through, physically or mentally.

For some, their body was lost in the war and their spirit returned. For others, even if their bodies came back home, their mind was still in the War. What started as Operation Homecoming ended as another lost battle. Everything was still lying on the field of valor; still hiding in the trenches, waiting for the next enemy attack.

My last operation, my last battle, was not in the rice paddies of Vietnam, but rather, on the telephone when I returned home. A Marine had died, Gary O'Brien, a good friend. I was trying to navigate the best way to handle the situation. Their son wanted to fight with machine guns and he wanted to represent his country; fulfill his civic duty through combat. I had spoken to the Captain and requested their son's right of passage. When it was granted, I never thought it would be a passage to death.

The courage it required, *the* call, the angst, the constant wondering of whether or not I would be received and whether or not they would want to talk, that moment was finally here. The ringing stopped.

"Hello?"

"Hello, I am one of the Marines that fought alongside your son when he was killed in Vietnam. Maybe I can help, maybe I can answer any questions you may have. If I could speak to your son's wife that would be great too."

240

"I thank you for the call. When you left the message you would be calling back, I asked my daughter-in-law if she wanted to speak to you. She has moved on...we all have moved on. But we thank you for the call."

Hanging up, I felt unsettled. I was happy to hear they had moved on, but I was perplexed as to why I felt dissatisfied from the conversation. People were moving on and continuing with life, but I wasn't. I couldn't move on. I didn't obtain the closure I was so desperately seeking. The call was as much for me as it was for them; it was to be a release of emotions that would never come.

You're finally home, it's a beautiful day and the sun is shining. You think you've left the war far behind you, in another time, in another world, but it's only an illusion. What should have been a simple, relaxing day at the mall with the wife you've missed dearly, turns into a war zone as you fail to notice the construction sign while traversing the plethora of stores. The sound of the jackhammer triggers the instincts that have now become deeply ingrained in every muscle fiber of your body; you forcefully pull your wife to the ground, frantically searching for cover in your exposed position; your only thought: *it must be an ambush.*

The sounds, the images of war, they never stop.

When I hear the sound of a helicopter's rotor blades overhead, I am instantly transported to Vietnam. My mind, flying over the tree canopies, on its way to another LZ, headed to another battleground, is in the middle of the jungle wondering who will die today. My thoughts swiftly interrupted with the trauma from loading mangled bodies of friends into a medevac chopper as it lifts off from a hot LZ; friends that I'll probably never see again.

FRONTLINE BROTHERS

On the battlefield, blood smelled the same to every Marine, fear felt the same, survival was the game, and death...death you will never forget. These are the aspects of war that stay with you forever.

During World War I, it was called shell shock. World War Two, called it battle fatigue. With Vietnam, they called it Post Traumatic Stress Disorder. Whatever name you want to give it, doesn't change the fact that young men and women are being sent into war without truly understanding the psychological consequences they will suffer if they make it home.

I sleep on a bed that transforms into a battlefield at night. With a pillow tactfully positioned on each side to prevent any escape, my efforts prove to be unsuccessful as I strike my head yet again, on the nightstand beside my bed. The battle never ends, there is a constant war inside my head.

Ironically enough, my entire life since Vietnam has been an attempt to get back that feeling I had on the battlefield. The sense of brotherhood, the esprit de corps, the focus; things were simple. You just had to survive. There was no past or future, just a battlefield. As bizarre as it sounds, I was happiest when I was on that field.

For years I stuffed Vietnam in a box and put it away. Then slowly, over time, as I began to share war stories, I recognized how those experiences shaped who I had become. Once I started talking about Vietnam, it was hard to stop, maybe because for many years, the topic had been so taboo.

When asked why after 50 years I wanted to tell my story now, my answer is simple: we need to be reminded about the price of freedom. Many have forgotten what commitment to our country and one another means. We have forgotten to remember those who died for our freedoms and sacrificed

242

everything so we may live. The newer generations of young people, many of which have never heard of Vietnam or learned about this part of our nation's history, need to understand the lesson behind it, so that history may not repeat itself.

The Vietnam War can certainly be called the first televised War. During the Korean War only 9% of U.S. households had televisions, but by the time the Vietnam War started, 85% of households watched the War from their living rooms.

The legacy of the Vietnam War is still questioned 45 years later. Textbooks and education rarely reflect the war as a major loss for the military and our government. Most Americans now, looking back, agree that it was a war not worth fighting; a war we couldn't have ever won. Many politicians and policy makers argue that we didn't do enough and could've been successful had we approached the war with different tactics. These misled thoughts have only allowed future politicians with even larger platforms to perpetuate this pattern, leading us into countless wars with no true objective. We have only to look at Iraq and Afghanistan as examples, our entry and exit speak for themselves as a clear indication for the mistakes they were.

The War Inside My Head

At night when I'm in bed,
the fight goes on inside my head.
Was surviving a mistake?
Now I'm trying to escape.
Did I really save his life?
What in turn would be the price?
Why did I keep the ring?
Did I really do the right thing?
Do I have to watch as he takes his last breath?
Do I still have to see all the death?
How long do I have to see the bullet going into his head?
How long do I have to lay among the dead?
Was that bullet meant for me?
How long do I have to wait to see?
Has my life been for those I left behind?
Has this really been for all mankind?

9.2 *Full Circle*

Lance Corporal Daniel Yeutter was the first Marine shot on the morning of June 2, 1967, during Operation Union II. He was one of the Marines that I attempted to save on that day. Dan was shot across his chest with his wounds sucking air. When I put cellophane from c-ration cigarette packages on the blood smeared holes, I prayed that he would survive, and by some miracle, he began breathing again. For over 50 years I relived that day a thousand times. I wondered if my efforts had succeeded. Was he still alive?

After Union II, PFC Mike Hernandez still had eight months left in Vietnam. Sometime during the month of August 1967, after Union II, Mike was sitting in his squad hooch at An Hoa, when in came Corporal Daniel Yeutter. He sported bullet scars on his chest and one on his arm above his elbow. He believed that nothing else would happen to him since he had already been shot so he saw no harm in continuing to fight and just so happened to be reassigned to the same squad as Mike Hernandez.

Mike and Dan both had a sense of humor and liked doo-wop songs; they quickly became close friends. He would ask Mike about Texas and Mike would ask him about Philadelphia, their home states. They talked about their families and things they had in common, allowing some reprieve from the monotony of war.

Later on, during the beginning of October, they rotated back to the coal mines. During perimeter watch, outside the bunkers on the western slope, they smoked cigarettes and sang doo-wop together. They talked about visiting each other's families when they got back to "the real world." During his time in Vietnam, Mike had been in fire fights with sniper fire hitting all around him, shrapnel flying from all directions; he survived Union II, saw many Marines die, and loaded more bodies onto medevac choppers than he could count. And he still had five months left. Amazingly, he had never been wounded. Union II gave him time to think about "buying it," a term that was used for getting killed.

On October 25 and 26, Fox Company was on a search and destroy sweep northwest of An Hoa. On the night of October 26, his company received small arms and rocket fire. Artillery was called in to a nearby village where it was believed the rocket fire had come from. The next morning, two squads with M-60 guns were sent out to the village where the artillery was called in. Lance Corporal King was on point, followed by Dan Yeutter, Mike Hernandez, Radioman Smitty, PFC Dominic, Lance Corporal Manciaz, Doc Aparieio, Felix "Speedy" Gonzalez, Lance Corporal David Wise and the M-60 machine gunner, PFC Moreno. They zigzagged through a series of rice paddies to get to the village, receiving only sporadic sniper fire. Upon reaching the village, no one was found. Only damage throughout the village from the artillery.

Once the village was cleared, the company turned back towards the perimeter at An Hoa. Halfway back to the perimeter, Lance Corporal King was again, walking point. King came to a knoll that connected the rice paddy to their front. King managed to climb up, but Dan Yeutter was having trouble. Mike Hernandez ran up and placed his hands together to make a step for Yeutter. As Mike attempted to boost Dan up onto the rice paddy, both Marines were instantly blown backwards, landing in the warm paddy water below. One of them had triggered a M-16A2 type landmine called a "Bouncing Betty," the same type of landmine that had given Corporal Barnes his first Purple Heart and took the leg of the Corpsman in front of him.

As Mike lay there, he realized he couldn't see or hear. His first thought was, *I'm dead.* As he struggled to get back up,

Mike felt hands touching him. He heard faint voices saying, "Stay down!" Mike could feel hands putting bandages on his head and other parts of his body; he lay there waiting for the medevac. PFC Dominic leaned down and hollered in his ear, "Tell the Corps not to send you back to Vietnam!" He then felt someone putting things in the pockets of his fatigue trousers. Some of the Marines had placed Vietnamese currency in his back pocket and Lance Corporal Manciaz had taken off his crucifix and put it in Mike's back pocket as well. As the medevac chopper landed to load him up, Mike could hear the rotor blades, but couldn't see them. When the medevac lifted off into the air, Mike could hear heavy breathing next to him, but was still disoriented.

When the helicopter landed at the Surgical Combat Hospital, he recalled a flashlight being shined into his eyes, but could only make out a blurred, faint light.

Later that afternoon, Lance Corporal King showed up at his bedside and told him they were transferring him to a hospital ship, but he didn't have any money. Mike told him to get the money out of the back pocket of his fatigue pants and asking King about the other Marines. King told Mike that he and Yeutter had both been brought in with him, but he didn't know Yeutter's condition. He wished Mike the best of luck and that was the last time Mike ever saw King. Mike was sent on to a military hospital in Guam. It was there that doctors removed the bandages. He was told he had lost his right eye and had blurred vision in his left. He suffered superficial burns on his face with numerous shrapnel wounds. A large shrapnel scar was on his right arm and a large wound was on his right leg. Additional scars peppered the rest of his body.

While at the Guam Military Hospital, he was able to have a Red Cross worker write a letter to his mother. He wanted to let her know that he was all right and not to worry about him. Mike eventually found himself back in California at the Balboa Naval Hospital in San Diego. He received an artificial plug in his right eye socket with plastic surgery done to his facial scars. Additional surgery was needed on his left eye where more shrapnel was removed. The sight in his left eye began to improve, but he still had residual blurry vision.

While at the Balboa Hospital, he was in the lobby when he saw the back of a Marine's head and he thought it might be Lance Corporal John Muth. He yelled, "Muth!" and the Marine turned around. It was good to see someone from Nam and the Fox Marines. Mike asked Muth about all the guys. He said Sergeant John Malone and Figueroa had been killed and he didn't know about Manciaz or Moreno. Muth went on to say that the NVA had overrun Hue City and the Fox Marines were one of the companies sent in to retake it. He said it was bad and a lot of Marines were KIA or WIA, including himself. Mike finally asked his burning question, "Have you heard anything about Corporal Dan Yeutter?"

Muth solemnly looked Mike in the eye, "Corporal Daniel Yeutter died in a military hospital from the wounds he received on October 26." It was the same day Mike had been wounded in the Vietnam rice paddy.

---

50 years later, I received this news and learned the story of Yeutter's fate during a phone conversation with Mike Hernandez, while gathering information for this very book. It was in this moment that I knew the battlefield, the war, these men, and their stories, truly had come full circle.

EPILOGUE

For the past 50 years I wanted to document my experiences in Vietnam, but as I'm sure most people can relate, life got busy! Between jobs and children and all the things that fill the spaces in between, I never found time to reflect on the past. And the one event in my life that kept resurfacing in different ways, ensuring those traumatic events were never lost in the crevices of my mind, was my time in Vietnam. My head was full of detailed memories; flashes of patrols, ambushes, and operations. Faces that flooded my thoughts and deaths that haunted my dreams. As I got older and my life allowed more time, I realized the importance of my story; I realized my new mission. My desire for this book was to not only leave my legacy for my children and grandchildren to read, but it was to also honor the many lives that were lost in such a horrific battle.

Once I decided to put pen on paper, I had to figure out where to begin. How do I tell my story and every other Marine's story? Every Marine in Fox Company, every Marine that fought, lived and died on those battlefields. How can I do them justice? I had my own memories, collection of articles, hand-written letters and opinions of how I perceived the war. But how different was my perception from theirs? Or was it? In order to tell more than just my story, I had to start contacting veterans who fought alongside me.

The first dot on my blank piece of paper began with a phone call to Corporal Brent "Mac" Mackinnon. I'm sure you'll recall his name being mentioned numerous times during the battle of Union II. Brent had authored a book titled, *PTSD and Expressive Writing, Ending the War Within*. Reading his book made it clear as to why I needed to start mine and talking with him reinforced my reasons for writing it. Brent had spent a number of years counseling and helping veterans who returned home with PTSD. On one of his trips to the

Soviet Union to counsel veterans who were coming home from the war in Afghanistan, he met another author named Larry Heinemann, who wrote *Paco's Story*. There's a quote in his book that Brent referred me to and I have read it many times since, "Tell the truth. Tell the truth with your whole body. Don't spare the reader. You tell it. We killed plenty of people. I mean me. Me. Tell the terror and horror. The total waste of it. Put the truth in the readers' hands. Write a letter. Tell the truth to a real person here in front of you. She wants to hear your story. Tell it to her. I want to hear your story. Tell it to me." There were instances where I questioned describing the graphic nature that accompanies war, where I wasn't sure if I wanted to place the images that haunted my mind in someone else's, but that quote made me realize that if I didn't, I wouldn't be telling the authentic story that I should be.

My next phone call went to **Private First Class** Mike Hernandez. Mike was one of only a few survivors from the Second Platoon. He had taken a group picture of the Platoon only a month before Operation Union II and I was hoping to get his permission to use the photo as the cover of my book. Little did I know the impact that conversation would have when I picked up the phone. Not only did he give me his blessing with the picture, he inspired the last chapter of my book called, "Full Circle." Mike's story wasn't just about the injuries and death those Marine's suffered during battle, it was about closure for all of us. Sometimes we never knew if the brother standing next to us, the one we had plans with once we returned home, ever made it back. Knowing what happened, good or bad, gave us a sense of peace.

This book is more than a story about one Marine and his time fighting in Vietnam; it highlights a flawed system and poor bureaucratic decisions based on politics instead of humanity. Young boys were thrust into a war with no clear vision on how far the U.S. was willing to go in order to achieve a winning goal. As the political makeup of our government changed, so did our strategies and commitment to a successful end. As soon as the decision was made that the United States would not cross the demilitarized zone into North Vietnam, the armed forces should have been pulled out. North Vietnam left their front door wide open and we failed to enter it. Lest we forget, history will repeat itself, as would happen 45 years later when the United States pulled out of Afghanistan. The images would become another Siagon.

There is no benefit to prolonged warfare, only universal pain and suffering. There is no benefit to hasty decisions and money-hungry politicians, only broken confidence in knowing that the rifle issued to you by your superiors would likely fail as you charged a machine gun bunker. There is no benefit to a lost cause except that your new mission is to ensure the survival of the brother standing next to you. And that's what these Marines fought for. They fought for the survival of one another and nothing more.

The last dot on my paper took me back to the first. Days and weeks passed as words were placed on paper, memories were recalled, phone calls were made, emails sent and information was gathered. The words had begun to curve; forming sentences, paragraphs and chapters, truly coming full circle as they rounded the pages. Learning what I've learned, not just about my fellow Marines, but about myself as well, has been beyond enlightening. It has given me a purpose and has helped me complete a mission I never knew I had until now. The amount of research, interviews, and documentation that went into this book, makes me proud to publish it. I feel confident that I have done the best that I could possibly do to ensure the reader experiences my war as well as the war of my comrades.

AUTHOR BIOGRAPHY

Rick Barnes served in the United States Marine Corps from 1965 to 1969. Attaining the rank of Staff Sergeant, he served as a Machine Gun Section Leader with Fox Company, Second Battalion, Fifth Marine Regiment. Rick fought 15 months in combat and was wounded twice in battle. He received the Silver Star, two Purple Hearts, the Presidential Unit Citation and a Meritorious Mast. Separated from the Marine Corps, due to his wounds, Rick returned to northwest Indiana. He went on to serve 22 years in law enforcement and graduated from the FBI National Academy. After retiring from law enforcement, he established a successful building and development company. Rick currently resides in Naples, Florida, thoroughly enjoying *true* retirement with his trusty pup, Havana, while he ponders his next book...

ACKNOWLEDGEMENTS & SOURCES

This book is a collaboration between myself and the men who populate its pages. I've based much of the narrative on my interviews, email communications and personal communications with the individuals who served alongside me. Going on patrols, operations, and ambushes in the jungles of Vietnam, I grew up with these Marines. We learned how to survive and die in a war long ago. I was a boy thrown into a man's war; having seen death and faced death when confronted with the atrocities of combat. Experiencing life in a way that most people never see in their lifetime.

The passages of these reconstructed dialogues came directly from interviews and credible sources of documentation. It is a memoir that recounts a narrative of unrelated short pieces. Each chapter describes a specific event as fragmented as the war itself. The resolution within these pages was to pursue only one objective, the conclusion of one's tour of duty. To arrive home in one piece with some hope of sanity.

In war, on the battlefield, in the jungles of Vietnam; a true non-fiction event can only be told accurately by the soldiers that witnessed it first-hand. Anything else is simply what someone was told through the grapevine, which we all know can be changed with time as it passes from person to person.

If you have 150 Marines on a battlefield, each one of those Marines will be involved in a different part of the battle, seeing and hearing different parts. Even the "After Action Reports" are not always accurate as they are simply recounts based on what the chain of command relayed to the admin clerk. One perspective may be different from the other simply because the experience itself was different, not because it was false. For that reason, it's important to acknowledge the fact that this book is not meant to discredit anyone or their story. It is meant to present the clear and convincing truth as authentically as possible, preparing our young men and women in and out of the military for life's many challenges.

Although in writing this book I consulted military after action reports and documents found in military archives, the most valuable sources came from the military authors themselves. The following people provided invaluable information towards the creation of this book and without them, its content would not be nearly as impactful or accurate:

- *Battlelines* by Lt Col David B. Brown (Ret.) & Tiffany Brown Holmes
- *PTSD and Expressive Writing Ending the War Within* by Brent "Mac" MacKinnon
- *Surviving The Claws Of The Tiger* by John Gobrecht
- *Highpocket's War Stories* by Col Pete Hilgartner USMC (Ret.) & Sam Ginder
- *Vicious Ambush At Vinh Huy* by Al Hemingway, www.namvets.com
- *Ambush at Union II* by Pat Haley, Marine Corps Gazette
- *Silver Star Marine* by Tom Willliams
- *Gallant and Intrepid* by Daniel Miller
- *The Worst Day* by Corporal Dennis Sheehy
- LtCol David B. Brown (Ret.)
- Sergeant Major Anthony H. Marengo (Ret.)
- Sergeant Hank "Ski"Januchowski
- Corporal Norm "Ozzie" Osborne
- Corporal Perry Jones
- Corporal John Gobrecht
- Corporal Brent "Mac" McKinnon, Navy Commendation Medal with Combat V
- Lance Corporal Terry Klein
- CPL Mike Hernandez

I want to acknowledge my brothers; my second family, the Marines that appear in my book and their families. Without them, their stories and their sacrifices, this book would not be what it is:

Colonial Kenneth Houghton (Navy Cross) 5th Marine Regiment ♦ Lt/Col Mallett Jackson 2/5 ♦ Lt/Col Pete Hilgartner 1/5 ♦ Lt/Col Charles Webster, 3/5 ♦ Lt/Col Dean Esslinger (Silver Star) 3/5 ♦ Lt/Col William Airhart 2/5 ♦ Captain George Burgett (Silver Star) Fox 2/5 ♦ Major Dick Esau 2/5 ♦ 1st/Lt James Scuras (Silver Star) Fox 2/5 ♦ 1st/Lt John Updyke 1/5 ♦ 1st/Lt Bill Link, Delta 1/5 ♦ 1st/Sgt Cleo Lee, Fox 2/5 ♦ G/Sgt John Green (Navy Cross) Fox 2/5 ♦ G/Sgt Sam Jones Fox 2/5 ♦ S/Sgt Tony Marengo (Silver Star) Fox 2/5 ♦ S/Sgt Sprimont, Fox 2/5 ♦ Sgt. Hank "Ski" Januchowski, Fox 2/5 ♦ Cpl Melvin Long (Navy Cross) Fox 2/5 ♦ Cpl Lloyd Woods (Navy Cross) Fox 2/5 ♦ CPL Rick Barnes (Silver Star) Fox 2/5 ♦ Cpl James Hester (Silver Star) Fox 2/5 ♦ Cpl Perry Jones, Fox 2/5 ♦ Cpl Chuck Conley, Fox 2/5 ♦ Cpl Brent "Mac" McKinnon, Fox 2/5, Navy Commendation Medal with Combat V ♦ Cpl Ted Verena, Fox 2/5 ♦ Cpl Pat "Water Bu" Haley, Fox 2/5 ♦ Cpl Tom Searfoss, Fox 2/5 ♦ Cpl Nutt, Fox 2/5 ♦ HN Wodja, Fox 2/5 ♦ L/Cpl Charles "Chuck" Barnes, Postal Division ♦ L/Cpl Ozzie Osborne, Fox 2/5 ♦ L/Cpl Gary "Astro" Asbell, Fox 2/5 ♦ L/Cpl John Gobrecht, Fox 2/5 ♦ L/Cpl "Mac" McAnnaly, Fox 2/5 ♦ L/Cpl Donnie Fountain, Fox 2/5 ♦ L/Cpl Dan Yeutter, Fox 2/5 ♦ L/Cpl Ken "Big Eyes" Reynolds, Fox 2/5 ♦ PFC Dennis Sheehy, Fox 2/5 ♦ PFC Terry Klein, Fox 2/5 ♦ PFC Tom LaBarbera, Fox 2/5 ♦ PFC Phil "Philly Dog" Hollens, fox 2/5 ♦ PFC Esquivel, Fox 2/5 ♦ PFC Robert Mills, Fox 2/5 ♦ PFC Cliff Nolan, Fox 2/5 ♦ PFC Jack Milton, Fox 2/5 ♦ PFC Legere, Fox 2/5 ♦ PFC Wainscott, Fox 2/5 ♦ PFC Johnson, Fox 2/5 ♦ PFC Mike Hernandez, Fox 2/5

Among some of the members of Union II that died on the field of valor, the following appear in Frontline Brothers:

Captain James Graham, Fox ⅖ (Medal Of Honor) ◆ Captain Ron Babich, Alpha ⅕ ◆ 2nd/Lt Straughten Kelsey, Fox ⅖ ◆ 2nd/Lt Charles Schultz, Fox ⅖ ◆ 2nd/Lt Larry Chmiel, Delta ⅕ ◆ S/Sgt David Dixon, Delta ⅕ ◆ Sgt Gerald Ackley, Fox ⅖ ◆ Cpl Gary O'Brien, Fox ⅖ ◆ Cpl Marion Dirickson, Fox ⅖ ◆ Cpl Victor Driscoll, Fox ⅖ ◆ Cpl John Francis, Fox ⅖ ◆ Cpl Karl Rische, Fox ⅖ ◆ L/Cpl James Deasel, Fox ⅖ ◆ L/Cpl Gary Kline, Fox ⅖ ◆ L/Cpl Jerry Westphal, Fox ⅖ ◆ L/Cpl John Painter, Fox ⅖ ◆ L/Cpl Robert Hernandez, Fox ⅖ ◆ L/Cpl Arthur Byrd, Fox ⅖ ◆ PFC Keith Moser, Fox ⅖ (Silver Star) ◆ PFC Micheal McClanless, Fox ⅖ ◆ HN3 Thomas Donovan, Fox ⅖ (Silver Star) ◆ HN Martin, Fox ⅖

The following are members of Union II that died on the field of valor and did not appear in this book due to their stories being known only to God:

L/Cpl Stephen Balters, Fox ⅖ ◆ L/Cpl Richard Blasen, Fox ⅖ ◆ PFC Larry Boatman, Fox ⅖ ◆ PFC Jimmy Crook, Fox ⅖ ◆ PFC Lawson Gerard, Fox ⅖ ◆ PFC Dennis Monfils, Fox ⅖ ◆ L/Cpl Benjamin Pelzer, Fox ⅖ ◆ PFC James Weed, Fox ⅖ ◆ L/Cpl William Daugherty, Fox ⅖ ◆ PFC Robert Richardson, Fox ⅖ ◆ PFC Steven Scharlach, Fox ⅖ ◆ PFC Clifford Shepherd, Fox ⅖

To those families and loved ones who lost their sons on the field of battle, I salute you.

The 17 men from Delta 1/5 who were killed in action on 02 June were:

2ndLt Larry V. Chmiel, Baltimore, MD
SSgt David L. Dixon, Marion, IN
Cpl Donald R. Christy, Yuba City, CA
Cpl Alejandro F. Fierro, Los Angeles, CA
Cpl Fidel Ramos, San Antonio, TX
Cpl Ralph E. Smith, Conyngham, PA (Silver Star)
Cpl Ray L. van Zandt, Austin, TX (Silver Star)
Cpl Kenneth R. Endsley, Sacramento, CA
LCpl Joseph S. Escobar, Fresno, CA
LCpl Joe Montez, Austin, TX
LCpl Joe Moya, Bloomington, TX
LCpl Fred G. O'Malley, Farmer City, IL
* Pfc Philip O. Parrish, High Point, NC
* Pfc Joseph J. Seller, Winsted, MN
* Pfc William A. Sinchak, Natrona, PA
* Pfc Neal R. Thalin, Dedham, MA (Bronze Star "V")
* Pfc Harold F. Werle, Roscoe, IL

The 18th loss was one of the four Navy Corpsmen who died that day - but we cannot determine which one it was.

CITATIONS

The President of the United States in the name of The Congress
takes pride in presenting the MEDAL OF HONOR posthumously to

CAPTAIN JAMES A. GRAHAM

UNITED STATES MARINE CORPS

for service as set forth in the following:

For conspicuous gallantry and intrepidity at the risk of his life above and beyond the call of duty. During Operation Union II, the 1st Battalion, 5th Marines, consisting of Companies A and D, with Capt. Graham's company attached launched an attack against an enemy occupied position with 2 companies assaulting and 1 in reserve. Company F, a leading company, was proceeding across a clear paddy area 1,000 meters wide, attacking toward the assigned objective, when it came under fire from mortars and small arms which immediately inflicted a large number of casualties. Hardest hit by the enemy fire was the 2nd platoon of Company F, which was pinned down in the open paddy area by intense fire from 2 concealed machine guns. Forming an assault unit from members of his small company headquarters, Capt. Graham boldly led a fierce assault through the second platoon's position, forcing the enemy to abandon the first machine gun position, thereby relieving some of the pressure on his second platoon, and enabling evacuation of the wounded to a more secure area. Resolute to silence the second machine gun, which continued its devastating fire, Capt. Graham's small force stood steadfast in its hard won enclave. Subsequently, during the afternoon's fierce fighting, he suffered 2 minor wounds while personally accounting for an estimated 15 enemy killed. With the enemy position remaining invincible upon each attempt to withdraw to friendly lines, and although knowing that he had no chance of survival, he chose to remain with 1 man who could not be moved due to the seriousness of his wounds. The last radio transmission from Capt. Graham reported that he was being assaulted by a force of 25 enemy soldiers; he died while protecting himself and the wounded man he chose not to abandon. Capt. Graham's actions throughout the day were a series of heroic achievements. His outstanding courage, superb leadership and indomitable fighting spirit undoubtedly saved the second platoon from annihilation and reflected great credit upon himself, the Marine Corps, and the U.S. Naval service. He gallantly gave his life for his country.

LONG, MELVIN M.
Sergeant, U.S. Marine Corps
Company F, 2d Battalion, 5th Marines, 1st Marine Division (Rein.) FMF
Date of Action: June 2, 1967
Citation:
The Navy Cross is presented to Melvin M. Long, Sergeant, U.S. Marine Corps, for extraordinary heroism while serving as Second Squad Leader, Third Platoon, Company F, Second Battalion, Fifth Marines, First Marine Division (Reinforced), Fleet Marine Force, Quang Tin Province, Republic of Vietnam, during Operation UNION II, on 2 June 1967. While advancing toward a designated objective, Company F came under an intense volume of enemy mortar, recoilless rifle, automatic weapons and small arms fire. Due to its exposed position, the Third Platoon was temporarily pinned down. Sergeant (then Corporal) Long was ordered to seize a critical piece of high ground in the tree line on the left flank. He moved his squad under intense enemy fire, across 200 meters of open, fire swept terrain into the tree line. With complete disregard for his own safety, he maneuvered his squad in an enveloping movement and assaulted the well-entrenched enemy position from the rear resulting in six enemy killed. Though painfully wounded, he led his men in overrunning the position and organized a hasty defense. From his newly won position, he observed another enemy machine gun position which was delivering accurate fire on the platoon. With complete disregard for his wounds and the intense enemy fire, he led another assault which resulted in two more enemy killed. He then organized a defensive position and defended their key terrain feature for three hours until the enemy finally withdrew. Upon learning of the enemy's withdrawal, Sergeant Long led his men to a landing zone some 600 meters to the rear and supervised the evacuation of his wounded. By his outstanding courage, exceptional fortitude and valiant fighting spirit, Sergeant Long served to inspire all who observed him and upheld the highest traditions of the Marine Corps and the United States Naval Service.

GREEN, JOHN S.
Gunnery Sergeant
U.S. Marine Corps
Co. F, 2nd Bn., 5th Marines, 1st Marine Division
Date of Action: June 2, 1967
Citation:
The Navy Cross is awarded to Gunnery Sergeant John S. Green, United States Marine Corps, for extraordinary heroism in action against enemy forces while serving as Company Gunnery Sergeant, Company F, Second Battalion, Fifth Marines, First Marine Division (Reinforced) in the Republic of Vietnam on 2 June 1967. During Operation Union II, Company F came under intense enemy small arms, automatic weapons and mortar fire from a well entrenched enemy force and was temporarily halted. Gunnery Sergeant Green, with complete disregard for his own safety, led a frontal assault against the enemy positions. Leading his men across 800 meters of open, fire-swept rice paddy, he quickly overran the Viet Cong machine gun position and personally accounted for ten enemy killed. After seizing the objective, he immediately established a hasty defense and began redistributing ammunition to his men. He fearlessly braved the intense enemy fire by exposing himself in carrying wounded to positions of relative safety. By his daring initiative, valiant fighting spirit and selfless devotion to duty in the face of insurmountable odds, Gunnery Sergeant Green was responsible in great measure for saving many of his comrades and thereby upheld the highest traditions of the Marine Corps and the United States Naval Service.

WOODS, LLOYD
Corporal, U.S. Marine Corps
Company F, 2d Battalion, 5th Marines, 1st Marine Division (Rein.) FMF
Date of Action: June 2, 1967
Citation:
The Navy Cross is presented to Lloyd Woods, Corporal, U.S. Marine Corps, for extraordinary heroism while serving as a Radio Operator with Company F, Second Battalion, Fifth Marines, First Marine Division (Reinforced), Fleet Marine Force, in Quang Tin Province, Republic of Vietnam, on 2 June 1967. During Operation UNION II, Corporal Woods' company came under intense enemy automatic weapons, small arms and mortar fire which temporarily pinned down the first platoon in an exposed rice paddy. In the initial burst of fire, the platoon sustained numerous casualties, including the platoon commander. Upon observing his wounded commander lying exposed to the intense enemy fire, he unhesitatingly ran through the heavy volume of fire to his side, placed him on his shoulder and carried him to a position of relative safety. Then, rallying four companions, he again moved across the open rice paddy to evacuate another wounded Marine who was lying in close proximity to an enemy machine gun position. Upon reaching the wounded man and realizing it was impossible to move him because of the enemy machine gun fire, he boldly maneuvered into the tree line towards the enemy position, and single-handedly assaulted the gun, killing the gunner and capturing his weapon. He then boldly leaped into the adjacent emplacement and, in fierce hand-to-hand combat, killed that gunner and commenced to fire the enemy machine gun against other hostile positions, providing cover while his companions evacuated the wounded man. As a result of Corporal Woods' courageous actions, his unit was able to regroup and succeeded in evacuating its casualties to positions of safety. By his intrepid fighting spirit, exceptional fortitude and gallant initiative, Corporal Woods inspired all who observed him and upheld the highest traditions of the Marine Corps and the United States Naval Service.

HOUGHTON, KENNETH J.
Colonel, U.S. Marine Corps
Commanding Officer, 5th Marines, 1st Marine Division (Rein.) FMF
Date of Action: May 26 - June 5, 1967
Citation:
The Navy Cross is presented to Kenneth J. Houghton, Colonel, U.S. Marine Corps, for extraordinary heroism as Commanding Officer, Fifth Marines, First Marine Division (Reinforced), Fleet Marine Force, in the Republic of Vietnam from 26 May to 5 June 1967. The Fifth Marine Regiment was launched on Operation UNION II to track down the remnants of the 21st North Vietnamese Regiment, which had been thoroughly decimated by them nine days previous. Responding to intelligence reports that the enemy was attempting to withdraw to the western mountains, Colonel Houghton committed two battalions in pursuit. The First Battalion swept overland while the Third Battalion was enveloped by helicopter near Cam La. The Third Battalion met with heavy resistance, but completely overran the enemy positions, causing many casualties. He was constantly in the operational area, bravely exposing himself to all the hazards of the battlefield. Colonel Houghton revised his tactics when intelligence reports indicated a much larger enemy force in the area, which was identified as the 3d North Vietnamese Regiment and pointed to a buildup along the Suio Cau Doi River, in the vicinity of Vinh Huy (2). Instantly reacting, he launched his attack from the east, with the First and Third Battalions abreast and the Second in reserve. On 2 June, the First Battalion came under intense enemy mortar, recoilless rifle and automatic weapons fire, indicating contact with the main force of the 3d North Vietnamese Army force. While the First and Third Battalions maintained heavy pressure on the enemy, he committed the Second Battalion to assault the enemy's flank. Although wounded at this time, he continued to aggressively advance on the enemy with renewed determination. Colonel Houghton launched a bold night attack which smashed through the enemy defenses, and annihilated the large enemy force. By his outstanding leadership, gallant fighting spirit and bold initiative, he contributed materially to the success of the First Marine Division, thereby upholding the highest traditions of the Marine Corps and the United States Naval Service.
Authority: Navy Department Board of Decorations and Medals

The President of the United States takes pride in presenting the
SILVER STAR MEDAL posthumously to

PRIVATE FIRST CLASS KEITH M. MOSER II, UNITED STATES MARINE CORPS

for service as set forth in the following

CITATION:
For conspicuous gallantry and intrepidity while serving as a Radio Operator with the First Platoon, Company F, Second Battalion, Fifth Marines during OPERATION UNION, in Quang Tin Province, Republic of Vietnam on 2 June 1967. While moving across an exposed rice paddy, the lead squad of the First Platoon had maneuvered to a position 200 meters to the front of the remainder of the platoon. The platoon came under heavy enemy small arms, machine gun and mortar fire from a well-entrenched enemy force. Private First Class Moser, realizing that the squad leader had no communications with the platoon leader, unhesitatingly moved across 200 meters of exposed rice paddy under intense enemy fire to provide the badly needed communications enabling the squad to receive and carry out its mission. After arriving at the squad's position Private First Class Moser observed a wounded Marine lying out in the rice paddy. With complete disregard for this own safety, he moved to the side of the wounded Marine and began administering first aid. Still under intense enemy fire, he started to carry the wounded Marine back to the squad's position. During this attempt, Private First Class Moser was mortally wounded. His daring actions and loyal devotion to duty and to his fellow Marines were in keeping with the highest traditions of the Marine Corps and the United States Naval Service. He gallantly gave his life for his country.

BARNES, LOUIS R.
Synopsis:
The President of the United States takes pleasure in presenting the Silver Star Medal to Louis Barnes (2150373), Corporal, U.S. Marine Corps, for conspicuous gallantry and intrepidity in action serving as a machine gun section leader with Company F, 2d Battalion, 5th Marines, 1st Marine Division (Rein.), FMF, in connection with combat operations against the enemy in the Republic of Vietnam on January 2, 1967. While conducting a search and destroy mission in Quang Tin Province during Operation Union I I , Company F was suddenly subjected to mortar , small arms and automatic weapons fire from heavily fortified enemy positions along tree lines bordering a large open rice paddy, temporarily pinning down lead elements of the second platoon and inflicting numerous casualties . Observing a wounded Marine lying in an exposed area , Corporal Barnes , with complete disregard for his own safety , unhesitatingly advanced under heavy hostile fire to recover his fallen companion and move him to a protected area. Displaying exceptional leadership and calmness under fire , he then skillfully maneuvered his machine gun team to a more advantageous position where it could deliver suppressive fire on the enemy positions while his platoon advanced. In an effort to silence Corporal Barnes' weapon the enemy shifted their mortar fire to his position. Although painfully wounded by mortar fragments , he steadfastly refused to leave his position and courageously continued to provide highly effective fire, enabling his platoon to complete its mission. By his courage, aggressive fighting spirit and steadfast devotion to duty in the face of extreme personal danger, Corporal Barnes upheld the highest traditions of the Marine Corps and the United States Naval Service.
Home Town: Highland, Indiana

HESTER, JAMES R.
Synopsis:
The President of the United States takes pleasure in presenting the Silver Star Medal to James R. Hester (2132683), Corporal, U.S. Marine Corps, for conspicuous gallantry and intrepidity in action while serving with Company F, 2d Battalion, 5th Marines, 1st Marine Division (Rein.), FMF, in connection with combat operations against the enemy in the Republic of Vietnam on June 2, 1967. By his courage, aggressive fighting spirit and steadfast devotion to duty in the face of extreme personal danger, Corporal Hester upheld the highest traditions of the Marine Corps and the United States Naval Service.
Home Town: Louisville, Kentucky

*DONOVAN, THOMAS S. (KIA)
Citation:
The President of the United States takes pride in presenting the Silver Star Medal (Posthumously) to Thomas S. Donovan (9132355), Hospital Corpsman Second Class, U.S. Navy, for conspicuous gallantry and intrepidity in action while serving as Senior Corpsman with Company F, Second Battalion, Fifth

and intrepidity in action while serving as Senior Corpsman with Company F, Second Battalion, Fifth Marines, FIRST Marine Division, in the Republic of Vietnam, on 2 June 1967. During Operation UNION II, while Company F was advancing toward a designated objective, it was taken under intense mortar, recoilless-rifle, and automatic-weapons fire from a well-entrenched, numerically superior enemy force. The company was temporarily halted in the middle of a large, open, rice paddy, sustaining numerous casualties due to extremely accurate enemy fire. Without hesitation, Petty Officer Donovan moved across the fire-swept field, heedless of the hail of bullets, to administer lifesaving treatment to the fallen Marines. After performing first aid, he then courageously carried several Marines to covered positions. When the Company Commander asked for volunteers to assault a machine-gun position behind enemy lines, Petty Officer Donovan immediately volunteered to accompany the group in order to treat casualties which would probably result from such a dangerous mission. Painfully wounded while treating an injured comrade, he nonetheless continued with his mission of treating the Marines and assisting them to covered positions until he was again wounded, this time fatally. Petty Officer Donovan's heroic conduct, selfless courage, and resolute devotion to duty were in keeping with the highest traditions of the United States Naval Service. Home Town: Natic, Massachusetts

The President of the United States takes pleasure in presenting the
PRESIDENTIAL UNIT CITATION to the

FIFTH MARINE REGIMENT (REINFORCED)
FIRST MARINE DIVISION (REINFORCED)

for service as set forth in the following

CITATION:

For extraordinary heroism in action against North Vietnamese forces during Operations UNION AND UNION II in the Que Son area, Republic of Vietnam, from 25 April to 5 June 1967. Throughout this period, the 5th Marines (Reinforced) was assigned the mission of destroying the enemy forces, their supplies and equipment. With the initiation of a heavy engagement by a Marine rifle company in the vicinity of La Nga (2), the 5th Marines deployed to exploit the contact.

Despite extremely short notice, the reinforced Regiment moved with alacrity to meet the enemy's challenge. This rapid reaction resulted in the establishment of contact with a well-organized North Vietnamese Army force; once engaged, the 5th Marines tenaciously pursued the enemy over an extensive pattern of rice paddies, hedgerows and fortified hamlets. Unable to disengage while being subjected to relentless pressure, the 21st North Vietnamese Regiment finally made its stand at the hamlet of Phouc Duc (4).

For four days commencing 12 May, the 5th Marines resolutely attacked the fortified enemy positions. Valiantly withstanding heavy enemy mortar barrages and repelling fierce enemy counterattacks, the Marines shattered the entrenched enemy. Operation UNION II was launched on 26 May with a helicopter-borne assault to destroy the withdrawing remnants of the 21st North Vietnamese Regiment.

Attacking aggressively, the 5th Marines uncovered the 3rd North Vietnamese Regiment dug in near Vinh Huy and were met by a withering barrage of mortar, machine-gun and recoilless rifle fire. Resolute in their determination, the Marines continued to maintain pressure and, at nightfall, launched a bold night attack which ruptured the enemy's defenses and drove the tattered vestiges of the North Vietnamese unit from the field.

UNION and UNION II inflicted over three thousand enemy casualties and eliminated the 2nd North Vietnamese Army Division as a combat force to be reckoned with for many months. By their aggressive fighting spirit, superb tactical skill, steadfastness under fire, consummate professionalism and countless acts of individual heroism, the officers and men of the 5th Marine Regiment (Reinforced) upheld the highest traditions of the Marine Corps, and the United States Naval Service.

The 3rd Battalion lost 38 killed and 82 wounded during Union II – May 26-June 2, 1967:

H&S Company:
    Capt James W. Ayers, Moncks Corner, SC
    HM2 John E. Schon, Portland, OR (Silver Star)
    HM3 Thomas A. Conklin, South Euclid, OH
    LCpl William R. Dalrymple, Hoquiam, WA
    LCpl Anthony J. Salerno, Cinnaminson, NJ
    LCpl Jerry G. Waller, College Park, GA
    Pfc Donald R. Troxell, Shelby, OH

I Company:
    LCpl Brock D. Elliott, Manteca, CA
    HN Edward D. Drohosky, Gary, IN
    Pfc Thomas G. Jones, Utica, NY
    Pfc Alexander G. Wainio, Troy, NH

K Company:
    Pfc William J. Bresnahan, Ashburnham, MA
    Pfc Michael J. Greeley, Milwaukie, OR

L Company:
    Cpl Anthony M. Cass, Artesia, NM
    Cpl Michael H. Collins, Tampa, FL
    Cpl Gerald F. McDonald, Dorchester, MA
    Cpl Benjamin Richardson, Detroit, MI (Silver Star)
    Cpl Joseph P. Smith, West Point, VA
    Cpl Allen W. Stath, Rensselaer, IN
    HM3 Laddie C. Stierwalt, Las Vegas, NV
    Cpl Arnold G. Wilkening, Spokane, WA
    LCpl Thomas R. Burns, Fremont, WI
    HN Michael W. Carey, Rescue, CA
    LCpl Lowell R. Lloyd, Woodlawn, IL (Silver Star)
    Pfc Dennis W. Frasier, St Johnsville, NY
    Pfc William G. Landon, Deerfield, IL
    Pfc Joseph Matthews, Chicago, IL
    Pfc Robert D. Millan, Southfield, MI
    Pfc Benjamin G. Mollica, Flushing, NY
    Pfc Jack Smaso, New York, NY

M Company:
    Cpl Roger V. Inscore, Huntington Beach, CA (Silver Star)
    Cpl James J. Menart, Mentor, OH
    Cpl John D. Rogers, Albuquerque, NM
    Cpl Charles A. Crump, Greenville, TX
    LCpl Harry K. Cartrette, Clarendon, NC
    LCpl Robert G. Goddard, Jenks, OK
    LCpl Allan H. Kellermann, Chicago, IL

(Note: This needs to be checked as I think some names are missing)

Made in the USA
Columbia, SC
03 February 2025

52606061R00143